2019

AI and Data Strategy

HARNESSING THE BUSINESS POTENTIAL OF ARTIFICIAL INTELLIGENCE AND BIG DATA

NIGEL SCHMALKUCHE, PETA MARSHALL AND REKHA SWAMY

Foreword

Through my 20 plus year career in the world of Information technology, I have read many books and hundreds of articles and papers to help me on my learning journey to get where I am today. I struggled to find books that helped me to apply the theory that was presented in many pages and would often have to figure it out myself.

I can tell you that it is very rare to come across a book that doesn't just tell you what you need to do, but how to go about doing it! The authors of this book have achieved a great balance between the theory and a practical approach to writing an AI and data strategy.

One of the measures of a good Enterprise Architecture book is the number of diagrams and useful information that you can lift and reuse, saving you oodles of time having to figure out what the authors' meant when they described the same in words. The examples of vision statements, principles, outcomes and stakeholder concerns are real life examples. I've seen them, written them, and used them on many projects myself, so having the authors give them to you in the book to use immediately on your AI and data strategy project, will save you time having to read through volumes of text and to create them yourself.

Many organisations fail to execute strategy because they overlook the 'People' aspects of delivering change. Transformational strategies like AI and data need to pay attention to how people's roles are changing and to invest in helping staff have simple, easy and enjoyable experiences at work. There are some good ideas that you can adopt in your AI and data strategy, for that matter, any strategy you write.

I am not a very technical person and I found it very easy to follow the ideas and advice that the authors provide along the way. This is a book that can be read by both technical and non-technical people. As more companies invest in digital transformations, AI and data strategies should be a key part of the transformation. Having access to a book such as this one, will ease your journey because it is comprehensive in guiding you in terms of what and how to invest in using AI and data to mature your business capabilities to achieve success.

Congratulations Nigel, Peta and Rekha! I can't wait for the next book.

Dr Christine Stephenson

Contents

Introduction

Klaus Schwab states in his book *'The Fourth Industrial Revolution'*, that *'We stand on the brink of a technological revolution that will fundamentally alter the way we live, work, and relate to one another.'*[1] This fourth revolution involves the blurring of the physical, digital and biological spheres and it is disrupting organisations at an exponential rate.

We live in an era where we are ladened with information, and this is the key to gaining rich insights about our world. Internet, social media and mobile devices have already contributed to the amount of data transmitted and shared across the globe in an unexpected way. There is now a new era of doing business which relies on data, where data-driven decisions result in better decisions. Being able to find more sustainable ways to improve quality and increase efficiency, or extract additional revenues through Artificial Intelligence (AI) and other emerging technologies is an almost irresistible proposition. In 2019, most of these technologies are still in their infancy but it won't take long for them to become a means of solving business problems.

AI can be utilised by organisations as a strategic capability to achieve positive transformational change when employees are appropriately skilled to use AI to innovate and reach business outcomes not previously possible.

Organisations need a clear AI and data strategy that is owned and supported by senior executives and understood by employees. AI and effective big data programs can increase operational efficiencies, anticipate customer needs, optimise prices, prevent fraud, promote innovation and contribute to sound decision-making through actionable metrics and data where businesses can execute their strategy.

---

[1] Schwab, K 2017, *The Fourth Industrial Revolution*, Portfolio Penguin, London, UK

One key thing that happens when organisations deploy effective AI and data strategies is that they understand that the human workforce must evolve to undertake more complex tasks once repetitive tasks are automated. If this transition is done effectively it can lead to a higher level of personal fulfilment as staff get to be decision makers and critical thinkers. Therefore, culture and organisational change are key to implementing an AI and data strategy outlining the play book for achieving cultural change and providing the way to deliver value realisation of the strategy.

Impact of Artificial Intelligence

Gartner research has revealed that the business value of AI reached $1.2 trillion in 2018 and is projected to take a massive leap forward, growing to $3.9 trillion by 2022.[2]

What is AI or Artificial Intelligence? It involves developing computer systems to perform tasks that normally require human intelligence. This includes visual perception like facial recognition, speech recognition, decision-making and language translation.

Will artificial intelligence cause the end of humankind? Will robotic automation take our jobs and turn half of us broke and unemployed? Or will humankind adapt, control and utilise these new technologies to improve the way we live and give us more freedom to pursue our pastimes. The latter is more likely.

In 1961, the USA President Kennedy said, *'the major challenge of the sixties is to maintain full employment at a time when automation is replacing men'*.[3] Human-kind has experienced many changes in the past and although the impact of artificial intelligence will be immense, we will be able to adapt to the change if we plan accordingly. This is true whatever industry you are in whether it is government, finance and banking, mining,

---

[2] Gartner Newsroom 2018, *Gartner Says Global Artificial Intelligence Business Value to Reach $1.2 Trillion in 2018*, press release, Gartner, Stamford, Connecticut, USA, 25 April, viewed 10 February 2019, <https://www.gartner.com/en/newsroom/press-releases/2018-04-25-gartner-says-global-artificial-intelligence-business-value-to-reach-1-point-2-trillion-in-2018>

[3] Nation's Manpower Revolution 1963, *United States Congress*, U.S. Government Printing Office, Washington, USA

agriculture, health and retail. Jobs where automation is possible are likely to be transformed and require less human involvement while there will be an increasing need for humans to do non-automated skilled tasks.

With knowledge of the changes coming with artificial intelligence, it is possible to stay ahead of the game and be able to carve out your future. Upskilling is essential and that is true whatever industry you are in; where you add or strengthen your skills and become technology aware. Leaders can play an important role in providing their staff with the opportunity to upskill and share the strategic vision of what skills they require to contribute to the success of the business or government agency.

Forbes said that the effects of artificial intelligence 'will change the economics of virtually every industry.'[4] Every company and every person that you know will use AI every single day even when they are not aware of it.

Machines are increasingly able to process information and perform actions that previously only humans could do. This ability is increasing at an exponential rate and the explosion of big data is one of the main reasons for this ability. Machines are easily able to learn tasks that are repeatable and can be programmed. The real advancement is in the ability of machines to learn through data collected automatically without human intervention. The incredible advances in AI are due to this different approach in teaching machines. It is called deep learning, where machines learn in a similar way to how we teach our own children.

Historically it has been difficult to program a machine to see the world the way we see it, but this has changed with the process of deep learning. For instance we can feed a computer thousands of photos of vehicles and the computer is able to determine the

---

[4] Kosner, A 2014, 'Tech 2015: Deep Learning and Machine Intelligence Will Eat the World, *Forbes*, December 29, viewed 3 February 2019, <https://www.forbes.com/sites/anthonykosner/2014/12/29/tech-2015-deep-learning-and-machine-intelligence-will-eat-the-world/#1114fad05d94>

different types of vehicles the way humans can see them. Self-driving cars utilising AI will change the face of many industries and this is all due to the deep-learning capability. The potential application of deep learning is endless across the medical field to recognise warning signs through viewing patient's eyes and the ability of law enforcement agencies recognising criminal's faces through social media.

Nick Bostrom in his book, 'Superintelligence: Paths, Dangers, Strategies', discusses the likelihood, timing and human ability to handle the rise of super-human-level machine intelligence.[5] It was enough for Elon Musk to tweet 'Worth reading Superintelligence by Bostrom. We need to be super careful with AI. Potentially more dangerous than nukes.'[6]

The jury is still out on whether AI will be able to possess some of the more higher-level skills that humans possess including thinking strategically, being inventive, imaginative or being truly empathetic and authentic to someone in need. The following image shows a grouping of the Superpowers of AI and Data that are emerging as game changes in the world. Here we consider how AI will encapsulate new technologies including the Internet of Things, as part of the platform where cognitive computing can operate independently to human intervention. In this way there are crossovers between each of the five groupings using AI.

[5] Bostrom, N 2014, Superintelligence: Paths, Dangers, Strategies, Oxford University Press, London, UK
[6] ElonMusk 2014, 'Worth reading Superintelligence by Bostrom. We need to be super careful with AI. Potentially more dangerous than nukes', August 3, Twitter Post, viewed 1 March 2019, <https://twitter.com/elonmusk/status/495759307346952192>

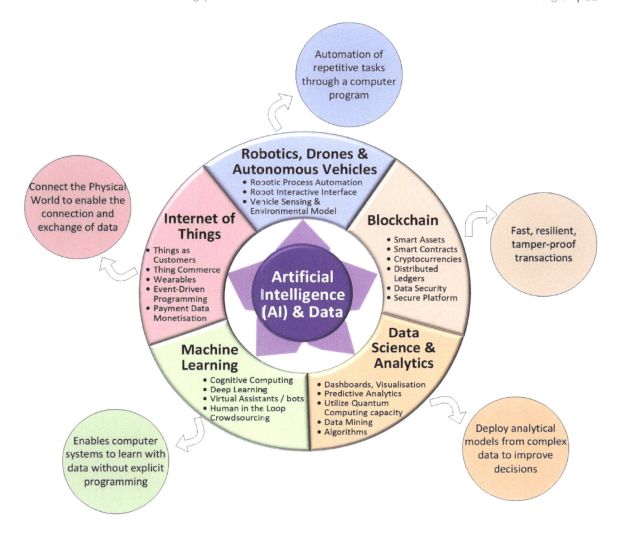

Figure 1: Superpowers of Artificial Intelligence and Data

The transformational potential of AI and big data is accelerating with the convergence of several technology trends. The world is awash with smart phones and volumes of data are increasing while costs to store data are ever decreasing. The five groupings above have been used as a base to describe the impact of major data and AI applications across business and society at large.

Internet of Things

The Internet of Things (IoT) is the base layer of where machine data comes from to support artificial intelligence through connected physical devices including sensors and electronic smart devices enabling objects to collect and exchange data. IoT devices are connected devices that produce data. This data is fed to their digital twins which are often their proxy, through which information is extracted and processed. By using analytical technologies insight from information can be gained to generate knowledge and wisdom to make business decisions. These disruptive technologies will touch every facet of our lives through smart homes, manufacturing, transportation, etc.

Machine-to-Machine communication is on the cusp of transforming business through processes that will enable an increasingly detailed digital representation of the real world for simulation, analysis and control. These things are expected to evolve further to impact a larger segment of the market and support a new phase of digital business.

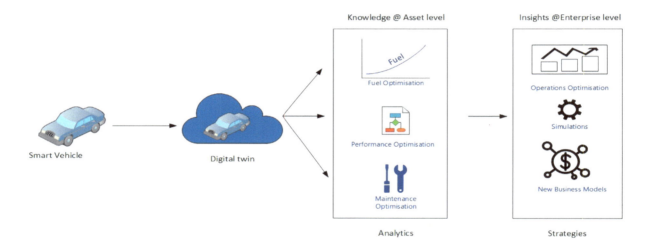

Figure 2: – IoT Data to Enterprise Insights

Machine Learning

Machine Learning enables computer systems to learn from data being provided through data retrieval mechanisms. They improve the ability of AI to function and better answer complex questions. Machine learning is a core part of AI that provides computer systems with the ability to automatically learn and continually improve based on that learning without human programming. Computers can analyse data, and learn from the data and information in the form of observations and continuous real-world interaction. Machine

Learning is enabling AI to become smarter and be more productive across every area of our daily life. Deep Learning is a subset of machine learning and has the potential to solve many world problems.

The IBM Watson application first learned to play the game Jeopardy but now plays a leading role in the medical industry, being able to, for example, efficiently read medical images.

Augmented and Virtual Reality (AR-VR)

Being able to interpret information from large data sets is a critical phase in the process of making meaning from big data. The following picture demonstrates the use of mixed reality Microsoft's augmented reality headset '*HoloLens*' glasses where it is possible to collaborate with others and utilise the inbuilt computing technology to see the world differently.[7]

Figure 3. Augmented Reality Glasses

---

[7] Roberts, J 2016, 'What is HoloLens? Microsoft's holographic headset explained', blog posting 30 March, viewed 5 July 2019, Trusted Reviews, London, UK, <https://www.trustedreviews.com/opinion/hololens-release-date-news-and-price-2922378>

AR-VR powered analytics help to turn the big data landscape into an area we can explore with our eyes. These immersive analytics enable the business to understand the data better if it corresponds explicitly with real content. For instance, to find a book among millions of others in the library requires extensive searching within a catalogue and the physical location. Powered with AR, users can see through the walls and shelves to look for directions e.g. red arrow showing the way. Big data visualisation can be enhanced if an AR-VR layer is overlaid on real-time streaming data or user context. What is limited by human vision, is enhanced significantly with the rich visual elements presented by AR-VR technology as in the following picture.

Figure 4: AR/VR Technology[8]

Blockchain

Blockchain enables fast, resilient and tamper-proof transactions to enable people who don't know each other to securely and quickly exchange products and services.

---

[8] Piletic, P 2019, 'Augmented Reality – The Future of Advertising', *Datafloq©*, blog posting, viewed 20 July 2019, <https://datafloq.com/read/augmented-reality-the-future-of-advertising/3333>

Blockchain has great potential to increase artificial trust and allow for data to be accessed more readily and sold through what s called data monetisation.

When the data is democratised or monetised, access and authentication could become a challenge. Security of big data becomes crucial because it continuously increases the exchange of sensitive data. Because big data utilises a complex distributed system where the main challenge is the complexity of managing a large implementation, new approaches to security are required.

Blockchain could provide that new identity system and authentication framework, which can be leveraged across big data technologies to ensure the security of the data. Blockchain-based identity presents a possible solution to replace username and password with a more secure authentication and access control. This identity system is similar to other Blockchain-based cryptocurrencies, such as Bitcoin.

Blockchain used in an authentication system creates a tamper-proof digital identity potentially to reduce the effectiveness of phishing attacks. Growing data and data hacks are strong indications that Blockchain is a very important technology that compliments big data quality and security, and will redefine the way data is distributed and shared. They promise a model to add trust to untrusted environments and reduce business friction by providing transparent access to the information in the chain.

Robotics, Drones and Autonomous Vehicles
Robotics, Drones and Autonomous Vehicles include many practical applications that will change the world. Robotic Process Automation (RPA) involves the automation of repetitive tasks that saves humans time. RPA is becoming more advanced, using image recognition and text analysis. Wikipedia says, '*Robotic process automation (or RPA) is an*

emerging form of business process automation technology based on the notion of software robots or artificial intelligence (AI) workers.'[9]

More CIOs are turning to RPA to eliminate some of the tedious tasks, freeing corporate workers to focus on work of higher value. RPA can be used in the process of extracting meaning from big data as it can provide analytical capabilities to examine the data across disparate information systems. For example, software robots using AI technology track and record their own actions, whether automating data entry, claims or order processing, or copy-paste tasks, as well as having the ability to gather information about customers. The analytical potential of RPA can be used to examine and make sense of the collected information. With the information provided from big data and the analytics provided by the RPA, it becomes exponentially easier for companies to gain insight about customers, business patterns, industry trends, and internal workings.

Data means nothing if it can't be understood, which is why major companies are looking to turn Data into Information, Information to Knowledge, Knowledge to Understanding and Understanding to Insight. Such knowledge and insights would be far better if they lead to thorough understanding. Previously unnoticed patterns would be given a physical presence, and viewers could absorb information with greater depth.

While written numbers can provide some knowledge, a 3D model allows everyone involved to see the information from all angles at once. For example, geospatial models that interact with big data can help city planners who study traffic patterns and other dynamic data. 3D modelling can bring multiple perspectives from a single experience. With the enormous amount of data growth, the demand for data storage would also increase. The storage devices developed through 3D printing are slowly becoming

---

[9] Roberts, J 2016, 'What is HoloLens? Microsoft's holographic headset explained', *Trusted Reviews*, blog posting 30 March, viewed 5 July 2019, <https://www.trustedreviews.com/opinion/hololens-release-date-news-and-price-2922378>

cheaper. The 3D printing market continues to grow with the speed of big data growth and it is expected to reach $21 billion by 2020.

Quantum Computing is an emerging technology that enables fast computing power to find innovation solutions to problems. Quantum Computing has the potential to revolutionise AI by the potential speed at which complex calculations can be performed. The new quantum-based approach could exponentially speed up big data sorting, cleansing and analysis. As the complexity and the sheer size of big data sets balloon year after year, one needs a way to process, organise, and extract true insights from the noise. Although major companies like Google and Microsoft are making considerable progress in this arena, there remains 5-10 years until quantum computing will be a feasible option for most enterprises.

The Importance of an AI and Data Strategy

To prepare for significant changes to business needs, a capability-driven AI and data strategy that identifies what is required to be competitive and take on future challenges, is needed.

Bernard Marr, a leading authority in AI and Data said, '*The starting point for any use of AI should be an AI and data strategy that identifies the biggest strategic opportunities and threats for any business and then pinpoints the most impactful applications.*' '*Simply experimenting with AI around the edges is not going to deliver the necessary effects on business success.*'[10]

This book provides the reader with a how to model with plenty of examples to allow you to grasp those strategic opportunities Bernard Marr refers to. A well-defined AI and data strategy can literally save organisations vast amounts of money and help define long-term strategic goals, as well as roadmap activities that will provide quick and medium-term

---

[10] Marr, B 2019, *Artificial Intelligence in Practice*, Wiley, Cornwall, UK, <https://www.amazon.com/Artificial-Intelligence-Practice-Successful-Companies/dp/1119548217>

wins to justify investment in the long term. To implement the AI and data strategy effectively requires a transformation that will influence the culture in the organisation and across data, information, knowledge, understanding and insight. This is illustrated in the following diagram and summarises some of the key concepts from this book.

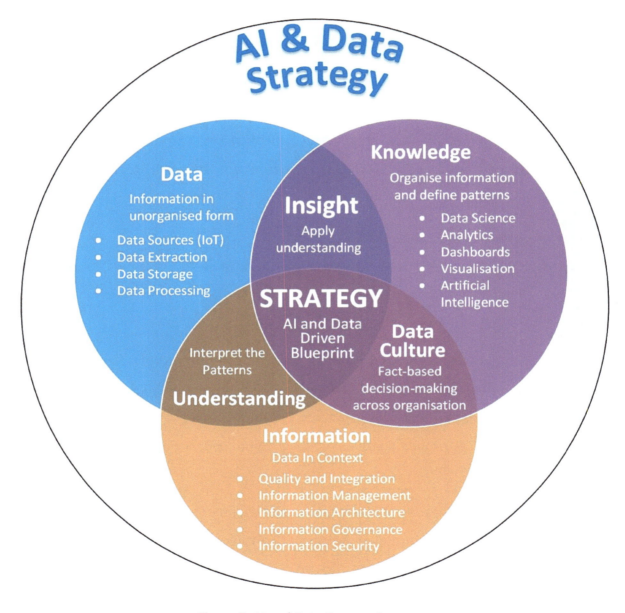

Figure 5: AI and Data Strategy Inputs

An effective AI and data strategy is necessary to bring about the transformation required to achieve the right culture in an organisation to maximise the use of the emerging AI and data technologies.

Chapter 1: Transforming Data to Insight

If big data has changed the way business operates, AI and emerging technologies are culminating the results to make the world more intelligent and wiser. AI and other emerging technologies are reshaping the expectations among Millennials and the youngest generational cohort, Generation Z. As we are beginning to see disruptions paving ways for innovative service delivery, enterprises are also beginning to realise the challenges of big data management. Nonetheless, companies, enterprises and even governments need to lead the development of innovative experiences through data, information, knowledge, understanding, and insights.

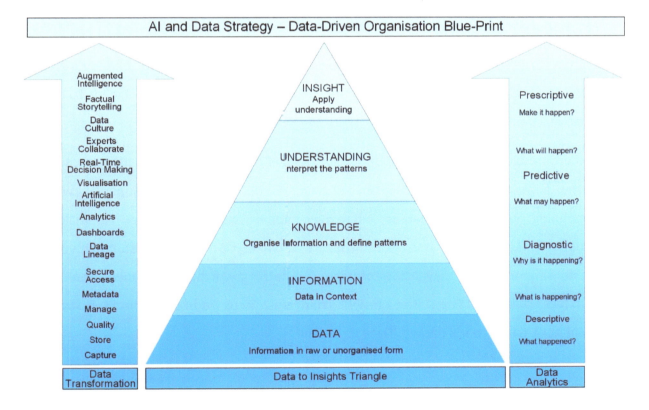

Figure 6: Data to Insight Triangle

The illustration above shows the need for a coordinated effort across all the areas of the Data to Insight Triangle, to deliver the AI and data strategy. The data layer includes the capture and store of data in an unstructured or structured form. The Internet of Things is within this layer as devices provide data and the data is stored for use.

The information layer provides context to the data, metadata classifications are provided to the data, information security is determined, and the lifecycle of the data is documented.

In the knowledge layer the information is organised and patterns are defined. It is here that data scientists apply analytics so that dashboards and visualisations can be applied.

In the understanding layer patterns are interpreted so that meaning is attached. Real-time information is applied, and factual narratives applies meaning to the statistics that are produced in the analysis.

Gaining Insight is the application of that understanding to a useful endeavour. The capacity for experts to combine their knowledge with the resources of AI leads to better decisions being made.

The progression in analytics to applying a high level of understanding is also represented in the diagram as we progress from reporting the following: what happened; what is happening; why it is happening; what may happen; what will happen; to making it happen. The progression mirrors the triangle as when you apply understanding you are capitalising on the data available to making something worthwhile happen, based on a high level of insight. The Data to Insight Triangle is discussed in more detail in Strategic Architect's earlier book named 'Data to Insight'[11]

---

[11] Schmalkuche, N & Swamy, R 2019, *Data to Insight*, Strategic Architects, Brisbane, Australia, <https://www.amazon.com/Data-Insight-Transform-Actionable-Insights-ebook/dp/B07MJVH8ZL/ref=sr_1_2?keywords=Data+to+Insight&qid=1549683057&s=Books&sr=1-2>

One of the key problems with big data projects is the obsession with technologies and tools, and lack of clarity and purpose with as to what the end goal is. This is an age where AI and big data are vital for business success, but there is also the potential for money to be lost in a data swamp unless objectives are clearly defined.

The ability to utilise cloud technologies has reduced the cost of data projects enormously, so that if the objectives are well defined, businesses will reap the benefits. Strategic Architects have found during workshops that if organisations do not embark on well planned AI and data projects they will miss out on the competitive advantage that other organisations are reaping rewards from. Consumers are expecting businesses to provide more tailored services to meet their needs now more than ever. This is critical to business survival.

The Art of Data Storytelling

It is important to understand patterns of data through providing quality visualisations that give appeal to data, and a narrative to give context. Insight allows for the application of that understanding and this could lead to greater revenue and profits; improved customer experience, engagement and loyalty that provides a return on investment for big data.

The missing link in data projects is to engage the decision makers through the art of storytelling, so they not only understand what is being shown, they can also obtain insights into how this new level of understanding can be applied. Daniel Kahneman was referring to data storytelling when he eloquently said, *'No one ever made a decision because of a number, they need a story'*.[12]

Data Storytelling is key to improving understanding and gaining insights. The following infographic gives some insight into the exposure of an example Data to Insight Strategy.

---

[12] Lewis, M 2016, 'How Two Trailblazing Psychologists Turned the World of Decision Science Upside Down', *Vanity Fair HIVE*, 14 November, viewed 4 November 2018, <https://www.vanityfair.com/news/2016/11/decision-science-daniel-kahneman-amos-tversky>

The simple infographic shows that, although the awareness of the strategy improved in the last three financial years to a very high 85%, only 5% of the ICT respondents would be able to explain the strategy in business speak.

Figure 7: Data to Insight Strategy Infographic – (Created in Canva)

Another aspect of this infographic is that it doesn't recommend an action to rectify the poor understanding of the strategy, but when telling a story, it is sometimes best to tell that story in stages and bite-sized chunks. A conclusion to draw from this infographic is that any future communication programs about the Data to Insight Strategy needs to include less technical terms so that it can be explained in practical terms. Before investing money in the communication program, this hypothesis could be tested and validated, and represent a repeatable pattern for future strategies and communications.

The ability to apply learnings from results is key to the improvement in data programs. Increasing data literacy in the organisation is essential to creating a data-driven culture, so any communication should begin to introduce well explained data terms that can take staff on the journey to become more data aware.

Making it Happen through Analytics

Figure 8· Information Analytics

With the various types of analytics, organisations are free to choose how deep they need to dive into data analysis to satisfy their business needs best. While descriptive and diagnostic analytics offer a reactive approach, predictive and prescriptive analytics make users proactive.

Traditional tools focussed on descriptive and diagnostic analytics, while new tools allow for predictive and prescriptive analytics by utilising machine learning and AI. It is with prescriptive analytics that you can make it happen. For example, prescriptive analytics can be of benefit to healthcare providers in their capacity planning, by using analytics to leverage operational and usage data combined with external economic and population health trend data. This combination of data may lead to more accurate planning for future capital investments such as new facilities or equipment, as well as the insight to understand the trade-offs between adding additional beds and expanding an existing facility versus building a new one.[13]

Prescriptive analytics will be the focus in data analytics in the future, as finance, marketing, supply-chain and retail sections of an organisation all demand a piece of the AI and data pie to improve business performance and stay ahead of the competitors. The combination of traditional structured information together with the unstructured information from social media through text analytics can be very powerful in achieving results. Human skills of imagination, creativity and strategic thinking can add to prescriptive analytics to make it happen and generate the outcomes required.

Big data will change the world and robotics will replace many low skilled jobs through automation, but we will be required to take conclusions produced by AI and add context so that good decisions are made. We need to evolve as AI evolves so we can harness its potential while excelling in all the ways that make us truly human.

An effective AI and data strategy will provide the direction needed to capitalise on the changes disrupting every business today, and in the future, and a culture plan to help transform the roles and perceptions of people into an AI effective organisation.

---

[13] Foster, R 2012, 'Big data and public health, part 2: Reducing unwarranted services', *Healthcare IT News*, May, viewed 22 June 2019, <https://www.healthcareitnews.com/news/big-data-and-public-health-part-2-reducing-un-warranted-services>

Realisation of the AI and data strategy will take a coordinated effort across the entire organisation and the lasting effects can transform the entire business.

Chapter 2: Strategic Alignment

The first step in developing an AI and data strategy is to examine the organisation's strategy in order to ensure alignment. This includes ensuring the strategic intent is communicated clearly so that the AI and data strategy delivers the organisation's strategy. This is ideally done by using the Object Management Group's business motivation model as a way to ensure alignment between the means to achieve the end vision.[14] The following figure shows how these concepts are related.

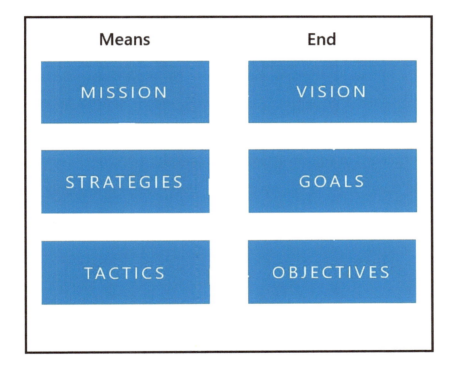

Figure 9: Communicating the means to achieve the ends

Utilising the organisation's strategy as a source of information before addressing the specific challenges in the AI and data environment has many benefits. Alignment is crucial to organisational success and an AI and data strategy that is far too technical that doesn't

---

[14] Object Management Group® 2015, *Business Motivation Model* v1.3, April, viewed 23 June 2019, <https://www.omg.org/spec/BMM/1.3/PDF>

embrace the organisation's direction will not be approved or funded by the executive. Alignment to other strategies is important as well, including people strategies, ICT, technology or digital strategies, service and operation strategies. The AI and data strategy needs to have tight alignment to the Enterprise Information Management strategy or include it as part of the AI and data strategy.

Capability-Based Planning

EA Learning provides training in Enterprise Architecture Certification in The Open Group Architecture Framework (TOGAF®)[15] and Business Architecture through their course Applied Business Architecture (ABA). The ABA course provides theory and practical examples of how to obtain this strategic alignment in the building of architectures in an organisation. The following diagram comes from the ABA course and shows how an organisation's capabilities of people, process, information and technology enable the achievement of the organisation's vision. The following Business Motivation Model[16] demonstrates the means to end chain, which was developed by the Business Rules Group. The diagram also shows how capability-driven architectures are designed to support the strategic objectives of an organisation.

---

[15] The Open Group 2018, *The Open Group Standard, The TOGAF Standard, Version 9.2*, The Open Group, <https://www.opengroup.org/togaf>

[16] Martin, C 2013,' The Business Motivation Model – a Key Tool for Talking Business', *EA Learning*, blog posting January 15, viewed 20 July 2019, <https://www.ealearning.com/resources/blog/the-business-motivation-model-–-a-key-tool-for-talking-business.html>

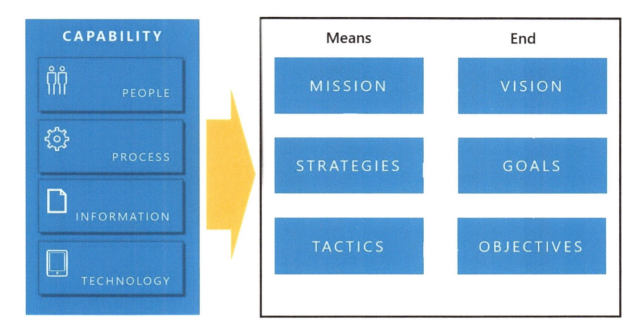

Figure 10: Business Motivation Model with Capability-Based Planning[17]

As trainers we conduct exercises in how to maximise the utilisation of the capabilities of an organisation to achieve strategic goals. The following diagram shows the alignment of the AI and data strategy to an organisation's strategic direction. When presenting the final AI and data strategy this can be important to show and explain how alignment is achieved.

---

[17] EA Learning© 2019, Applied Business Architecture Course, viewed 23 June 2019, <https://www.ealearning.com/our-courses/courses/applied-business-architecture.html>

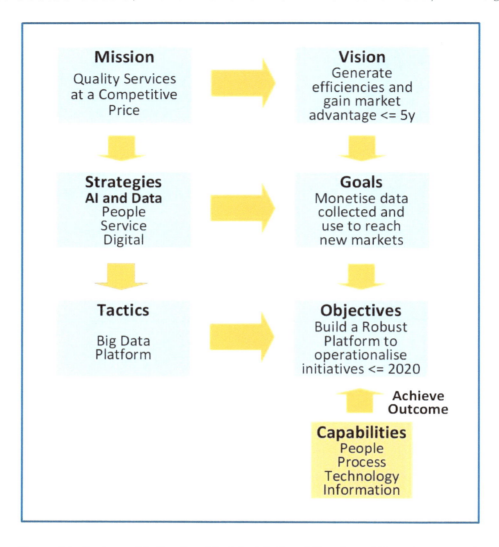

Figure 11: Business Motivation Model with Capability-Based Planning Example

Enterprise Architects are well placed to provide the linkage between organisational strategy and technology strategies and determine the drivers behind the strategy that is being developed. These drivers need to reflect the different perspectives that are across the organisation to achieve the strategic outcomes required.

AI and Data Drivers

There are four major drivers to AI and data: business, consumers, technology and finance.

Business	Analysing large data sets and gaining valuable insights through real-time analysis utilising AI and other technologies. This become the basis for competition and enable businesses to innovate in ways not achieved previously. Every company will need to enable AI to survive.
Consumers	Big data will enable companies to target smaller segments of the market with products and services that consumer groups have not had previously. Location-based services will alert customers to what they want, when they want it. AI controlled applications will make it far easier for consumers to get what they want from organisations.
Technology	Data science tools and techniques, the introduction of AI and the ability to store information cheaply in the cloud will revolutionise the entire ICT landscape, replace tasks that can be automated and enable insights through data analysis.
Finance	Efficiencies gained from the use of AI will gather steam as the implementation of AI becomes cheaper to implement. Big data and the tools that are used to process the data into meaningful insights in real-time will enable far better cost control than previously, where there was a significant delay in processing data.

It is important to ask what the key drivers are in developing the AI and data strategy as every strategy is different. They depend on which industry the organisation is in and what maturity they have in the market. This includes finding ways to innovate to discover insights, target customer groups, gain efficiencies through AI automation and gaining intelligence from utilising accurate data when required. With government, any of these drivers can be important with an overriding concern of delivering services better and more efficiently to customers.

Enterprise Architects' Strategic Leadership

Enterprise Architects are well placed to communicate to stakeholders across the organisation. It is the responsibility of the Enterprise Architect to stay abreast of the latest emerging trends and present a strategic architecture view on how these opportunities align to the organisation's strategy.

Strategic Architects are often called Strategic Enterprise Architects or Enterprise Architect Strategists as they apply a strategic view across Business, Information and Technology disciplines. The application of TOGAF® can be achieved by Strategic Architects through the implementation of a well scoped Request for Architecture Work as shown in the following diagram. [18]

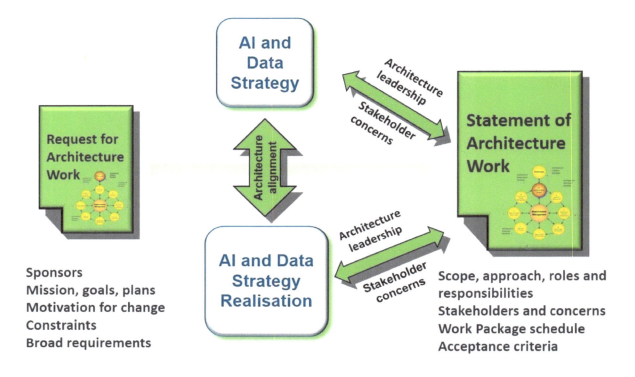

Figure 12: Enterprise Architect Strategic Leadership

Stakeholder Concerns

The previous diagram shows how the influence of stakeholder concerns or observations shape the architecture work to produce and implement the AI and data strategy. The following table shows examples of stakeholder concerns collected for the development of an AI and data strategy and associated implementation.

---

[18] The Open Group 2018, *The Open Group Standard, The TOGAF Standard, Version 9.2*, The Open Group, <https://www.opengroup.org/togaf>

Role	Stakeholder Concerns
Chief Executive Officer (CEO)	Turbulent change is challenging the organisation, leaving us unable to capitalise on opportunities
Chief Data Officer (CDO)	Fragmented, incomplete and inaccurate information eroding the importance of data to the organisation for decision-making
Chief Information Officer (CIO)	Organisation is primarily focused on the technology aspects of AI without focus on meeting business strategy
Strategic Architect	Unclear direction on how big data and AI is used and how they will meet business strategic goals
Organisational Change Manager (OCM)	Some people are frightened by the onset of artificial intelligence and cannot see their future
Business Manager (BM)	Data needs to be collected for the purpose of gaining insight to achieve business goals

Based on these stakeholder concerns, the next step is to identify which key outputs from the AI and data strategy, and the realisation of that strategy, will resolve the concerns provided. At this stage, these are the key outputs that the senior stakeholder will receive to address at a high level their specific concerns and helps justify their investment in the architecture work.

Key AI and Data Output	Description of Output	Outputs that will address Stakeholders concerns					
		CEO	CDO	CIO	SA	OCM	BM
Strategy	High-level plan to achieve overall aims	✔		✔	✔	✔	✔
Roadmap	Schedule of work packages with key outcomes				✔		✔
Data Culture	Workplace environment that embraces data	✔	✔	✔		✔	
Realisation	Long-term adoption of strategy	✔	✔	✔	✔		
Value Stream	Create a Value Stream to guide all AI and Data projects	✔	✔	✔	✔		✔

The Value Stream is a technique used in Business Architecture based on TOGAF.[19] The use of Value Streams and assigning the associated capabilities to achieve the value which is of most benefit to the organisation is workshopped in greater depth in the Applied Business Architecture Course run internationally by EA Learning.[20]

Here is an example of a Value Stream to address the stakeholder concern of the Business Manager as shown above: *'Data needs to be collected for the purpose of gaining insight to achieve business goals.'*

Figure 13: Data to Insight Value Stream

Value Streams are easy to develop and quite often can encapsulate what the stakeholder wants from the organisation's AI and data strategy. Establishing the stakeholder concerns and identifying what they require in simple and understandable language is vital in preparing the strategy. The value stream above can in simple terms frame the strategy as the business outcome of acting on insight is critical. In the next chapter, the strategic architecture template will be used to provide the steps to build the strategy, and provide very useful examples that can lead to the development of your own AI and data strategy.

---

[19] The Open Group 2018, *The Open Group Standard, The TOGAF Standard, Version 9.2*, The Open Group, <https://www.opengroup.org/togaf>
[20] EA Learning 2019, Applied Business Architecture, viewed 2 June 2019, <https://www.ealearning.com/our-courses/courses/applied-business-architecture.html>

Chapter 3: Building the Strategy

Strategic Architects have run AI and data strategy workshops that have revealed many different drivers and objectives from participants, depending on which industry they come from, and more importantly, which discipline they specialise in.

Although people have their own biases and views on what path to take, it is important to capture those views and collectively develop a strategy that is more well-rounded and will resonate with everyone in the organisation. This supports the data-driven culture.

What is Strategic Architecture and how can it be used to develop a Strategy?

The Open Group Architecture Framework (TOGAF®) defines Strategic Architecture as a *'long-term summary view of the entire enterprise'* and a *'framework for organising operational and change activity.'*[21] Strategic Architects have designed a template to develop ICT strategies with senior ICT and business leaders. Based on this implementation model, we define Strategic Architecture as a high-level enterprise architecture view of a Strategic ICT opportunity that aligns with the organisation's business vision and can be understood by senior ICT and business leaders. By undertaking strategic architecture, the Enterprise Architect becomes vitally important for the whole organisation and not just the ICT division. Strategic Architecture provides a template to develop an effective AI and data strategy that can be understood by ICT and business.

---

[21] The Open Group 2018, *The Open Group Standard, The TOGAF Standard, Version 9.2*, The Open Group, <https://www.opengroup.org/togaf>

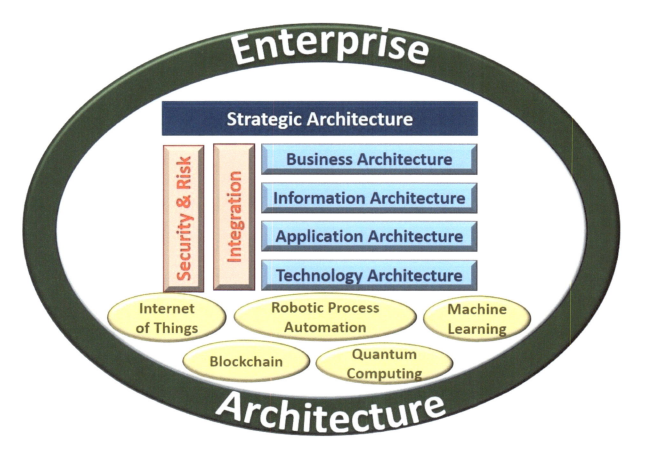

Figure 14: Strategic Architecture as part of Enterprise Architecture

In a traditional view of enterprise architecture there are business, information, applications and technology domains. More contemporary models include Integration, and Security and Risk Management domains across these traditional domains. Data is included in the Information Architecture domain. In the early days of Enterprise Architecture, during the 1990s and 2000s, the practice came from an application and technology focus seeking to remove the silos and guide organisations into working together to ensure collaboration and best utilise money spent on IT. This is still important, but Enterprise Architecture is increasing been seen as a business enabler.

Strategic Architects understand this and are principally concerned with showing how ICT can be an enabler to achieve business strategy goals and achieve outcomes required. Strategic Architecture represents the target architecture across all domains and provides the guidance needed so that all architectural efforts are focused to achieve organisational objectives and positive business outcomes.

Enterprise Architects can provide strategic leadership on a range of emerging technologies including the example five artificial intelligence technologies featured in the above diagram. In this chapter we will consider AI and Data in the development of a comprehensive strategy. However, depending on the impact on an organisation, specific strategies, discussion papers and technology positioning statements may be required for individual technologies. It is the responsibility of the Enterprise Architect to stay abreast of the latest emerging trends and present a strategic architecture view on how these opportunities can benefit the organisation.

The following figure shows a high-level summary of how to develop a strategy based on the Strategic Architecture template. It is important to work with senior ICT and business leaders including the Chief Data Officer or equivalent, and other senior Data and Information professionals in the development of an AI and data strategy. Running a workshop with these stakeholders is important to identify their concerns and obtain support and direction. Having a professional that has knowledge of AI and data to facilitate and guide discussions is essential to keep the momentum on track and provide the industry knowledge required.

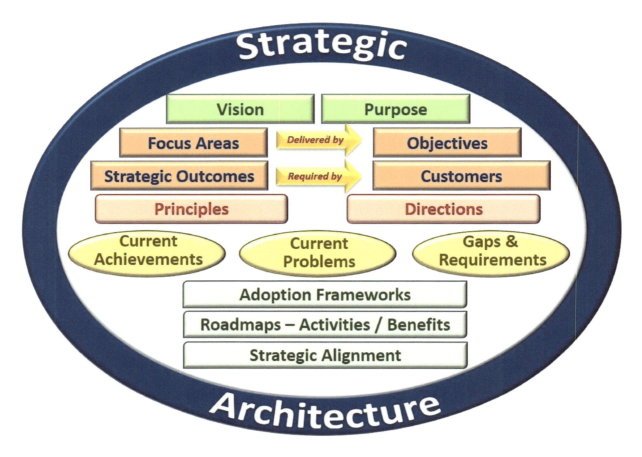

Figure 15: How to develop Strategic Architecture

Strategic Architects have found it useful, when time permits, to run a Business / Strategy Model Canvas adapted exercise, to change the focus of the participants from their day to day work related tasks to how AI and data will affect the organisation going forward. There are also many videos on AI and data that can set the scene for the workshop and for delivering the strategy when completed, to the executive and staff.

Strategies are specific to each organisation to determine where they are now, where they would like to be and how to get there.

We have run AI and data workshop strategy sessions with participants from all over Australia and New Zealand. From these sessions, it has become evident that each organisation is different, and each person has their own views and experiences. Examples from these workshops have been provided to help contextualise what is required in each step, and assist you in the process of developing your strategy for your own organisation. The goal of presenting these examples is to serve as inspiration in developing your own strategy.

The figure below provides an explanation of the major steps in establishing a strategy based on the strategic architecture template. These steps have been utilised for workshops in the development of AI and data strategies for organisations.

Strategies can also include mission, value and goal statements but they have been omitted in this chapter for simplicity. For AI and data strategies the eight steps outlined in the figure below, are the essential steps to set the organisation up for a sound strategy using the adoption framework provided.

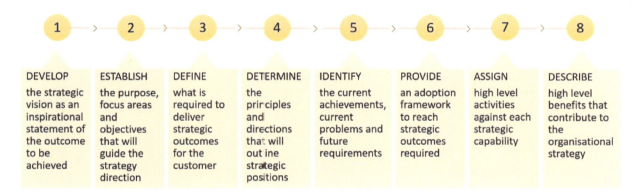

Figure 16: Eight steps in developing an Artificial Intelligence and Data Strategy

Vision

The vision is the first thing you read in a strategy and it must be inspirational, simple, clear and either directly or indirectly link back to the organisational vision and goals. Below are several example vision statements that we have brainstormed in workshops across government and business. It may be necessary with some organisations to define a mission statement for the AI and data strategy but in most cases linking the vision to the corporate mission is sufficient.

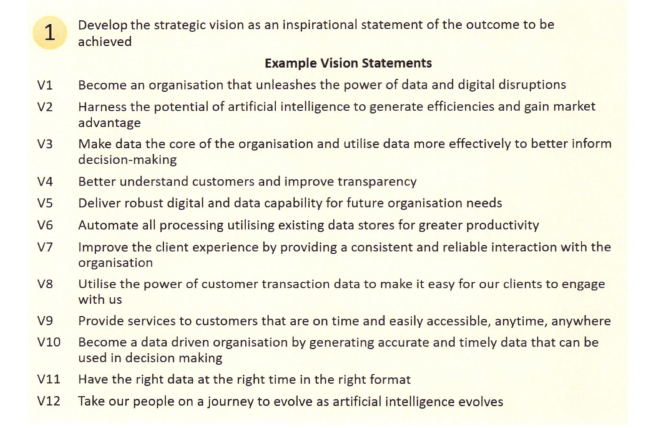

1 Develop the strategic vision as an inspirational statement of the outcome to be achieved

Example Vision Statements

V1   Become an organisation that unleashes the power of data and digital disruptions

V2   Harness the potential of artificial intelligence to generate efficiencies and gain market advantage

V3   Make data the core of the organisation and utilise data more effectively to better inform decision-making

V4   Better understand customers and improve transparency

V5   Deliver robust digital and data capability for future organisation needs

V6   Automate all processing utilising existing data stores for greater productivity

V7   Improve the client experience by providing a consistent and reliable interaction with the organisation

V8   Utilise the power of customer transaction data to make it easy for our clients to engage with us

V9   Provide services to customers that are on time and easily accessible, anytime, anywhere

V10   Become a data driven organisation by generating accurate and timely data that can be used in decision making

V11   Have the right data at the right time in the right format

V12   Take our people on a journey to evolve as artificial intelligence evolves

Purpose, Focus Areas and Objectives

The next step is to establish the purpose of the strategy, determine the high-level focus areas that encapsulate the result and define the medium-term objectives that describe how the focus areas will be achieved. For example, with a focus area named *'Proactive Decisions',* there could be an objective to establish a big data platform that would provide the AI and other technologies required to operationalise the capture of data through to the presentation of statistics that can be utilised to support decisions in targeting new markets. It is recommended to include goals and specific metrics within the strategy.

2 Establish the purpose, goals and objectives that will guide the strategy direction

Example Purpose Statements

P1 Provide a blueprint that identifies what is required to realise the vision of becoming a data driven organisation

P2 Gain community confidence and willingness to interact with the organisation

P3 Develop innovative solutions to improve citizen services

P4 Create a data driven decision culture to address citizen problems

P5 Build big data skills and nurture data science within the organisation

P6 Maximise customer delivery, service and insights to make easier and more informed decisions

P7 Build the necessary capabilities to improve the quality of service provided to customers

Example Strategic Focus Areas

G1 Improve Productivity

G2 Proactive Decisions

G3 Value Data

G4 Exploit Artificial Intelligence

G5 Integrate Processes

G5 Enhance Service Delivery

G6 Deliver New Market Opportunities

G7 Trust Data

G8 Value our People

Example Strategic Objectives

O1 To enable 10% more efficient usage of electricity by December 2019

O2 To manage the seamless flow of traffic and reduce accidents and incidents by 5% in 2019/2020 financial year

O3 To manage waste management more efficiently to reduce total cost of operations by 15%

O4 To build a big data platform that can operationalise data initiatives by June 2020

Strategic Outcomes

Strategic Outcomes are vital as it focuses on what is required and resonates with both business and ICT professionals. By collaborating with stakeholders to determine strategic outcomes you are more likely to be successful as it defines what is required.

In the next chapter we will discuss the need for the right mix of skills and structure to have a data culture that can provide an environment which delivers the strategic outcomes. Once the Strategic Outcome for the business is defined this can be matched with the required technology. For instance, Self Service may be provided by business intelligence, analytics, reporting or visualisation tools like Microsoft Power Bi, QlikView or Tableau. The selection of appropriate technology to deliver the strategic outcome may be part of a complete tendering process for the entire big data platform, a proof of concept, or a procurement of individual technologies to establish the most important capability that is required. The establishment of an Insight Community of Excellence is a means of creating a collaborative community of experts to stocktake what is existing in the organisation, advise on the correct path to take, showcase successes in the organisation, and assign responsibilities to datasets.

The following table provides some example strategic outcome statements for inclusion in the AI and data strategy.

3   Define what is required to deliver strategic outcomes for the customer

Example Strategic Outcome Statements

Self Service	I have the flexibility to choose the appropriate analysis and visualisation tool and select my own specific data for analysis that is accurate, relevant, supported and secure. I can access trusted data in my own business domain and simulate situations to develop my own business insights
Analytics	The right analytics method is available for the right situation so I can be proactive and prescriptive in my decision-making to achieve goals
Automation	Automate the way data is collected (devices, sensors and systems) and the way data is stored, processes, analysed and presented
Quality	Ensure data is reliable and fit for its possible use in operations, decision-making and planning
Integration	Integrate systems that have customer data through common identifier, while ensuring consistent data cleansing across data channels
Governance	Govern data effectively with assigned data stewards to provide a high level of confidence in data integrity and support strategic goals
Intelligence	Utilise artificial intelligence where it can improve the speed of processing, accuracy, value or help visualise information better for experts to make decisions
Storytelling	Give data the right context to facilitate the best decision
Engine	Provide assessment rules engines, risk proofing engines, identify profiling engines, known cloud engines
Culture	Create an environment where it is accepted that every decision is made from quality data from proven algorithms
Transition	Re-training is a priority so our people are equipped to have the right skills to harness the potential of artificial intelligence

Principles and Directions

Principles are important as they are unambiguous statements that are the foundation of the strategy. A good example of a principle in an AI and data strategy is that there must be a 'single source of truth for data'. This leads to the provision of accurate data for self-service that is listed as a strategic outcome above. Directions are clear and concise statements that specify the organisation's preferences and can be further explained in a policy, guideline or procedure. For instance, a direction can further explain the cloud-only principle by specifying SaaS, public cloud option as the first option for all new AI and data technologies, providing that the data sets do not contain protected information. In this situation a private cloud could be established. The strategic architecture template contains principles and directions as ICT strategies require a high of level of understanding to be accepted by ICT and business leaders. Below are some sample principle statements for an AI and data strategy.

4   Determine the principles that will outline strategic positions

Example Principles

Single Source	Maintain single source of truth repositories with the ability to present data in multiple ways and ensure that the single source is utilised for workflow and reporting
Fit for Purpose	Investment must deliver value and benefits and the right technology is used to solve the defined problem
Customer is King	Capture information only at first point of contact with customer, build a complete view by recognising related data for same customer and provide clients with the data they require.
Stewardship	Each data set must have a data steward and they are responsible for data accuracy
Cloud Only	All technologies procured in building the big data platform and procuring artificial intelligence technologies must be cloud only to allow for the latest features and the greatest capacity
Analytics First	Analytics are the spine of the organisation where decisions must be evidence-based made on quality data utilising algorithms developed from analytics methods
Accountability	Roles, responsibilities and accountabilities should be clearly defined
Managed	Information must be accurate, relevant, timely, available and secure
Outcome Focus	All data and artificial intelligence projects must have clearly defined problems and focused on achieving an outcome
Beneficial AI	All AI projects must be undertaken based on research that will benefit the organisation

Current Achievements, Current Problems and Future Requirements

It is important to list current achievements, problems and future tasks or requirements. These can be simply listed under the headings *'What have we achieved'*, *'What problems do we still need to solve'* and *'What do we need to do'*. As a senior manager there is nothing worse than reviewing a strategy that does not articulate what has been achieved by the area to date. They need to know what their existing investment has achieved before approving strategies and plans that require more investment.

5 Identify the current achievements, current problems and future requirements

Example Current Achievements

A1   Basic business intelligence, analytics and reporting tools associated with systems utilised

A2   Various data science and analytics initiatives in operation independently across organisation

A4   Batch data utilised effectively for reports providing corporate metrics for KPIs

Example Current Problems

P1   No real / time streaming of data

P2   No self-service to interrogate your own data and gain insights

P3   No big data platform to operationalise successful data science and analytics initiatives

P4   Limited emphasis on data quality that has led to a lack to trust in reports and dashboards

P3   Lack of Data Culture with most decisions based on 'gut feel' rather than fact

P4   Lack of data to make sound budgeting estimates

P5   Significant time spend on re-keying between systems, validation and reconciliation rather than analysis

Example Future Requirements

F1   Implement self-service portals with your choice of analytical tools fit for purpose

F2   Build a big data platform for cross application analytics and reports, collaboration and real-time display

F3   Provide the tools and techniques for our people to evolve as artificial intelligence evolves

F4   Implement successful predictive models based on proven data science algorithms

F5   Utilisation of artificial intelligence to apply digital transformation and deliver solutions at speed

F6   Establish an Insights Community of Excellence and encourage the sharing of successful data science initiatives and sound data practices

F7   Create a centralised data store (data lake) for structured and unstructured data and establish sound information governance so all data sets have information stewards

Adoption Framework

The adoption of an AI and data strategy in a medium to large organisation is a sizeable undertaking. The remainder of this book discusses the need for capabilities to develop across the whole of the data to insight triangle in an organisation to be able to deliver on the expectations created by the strategy.

There are several studies that identify a high failure rate in achieving strategy success. In a 2006 global study, The Monitor Group asked senior executives about their priorities and number one, by a clear margin was implementing the strategy.[22]

Figure 17: Strategy Adoption Framework Stages

The adoption framework stages indicate a linear process, but often the stages commence earlier than shown in the diagram.

The adoption framework stages begin with governance as any data initiative must start with assigning the responsibilities to obtain ownership of data sets and establish data quality. This includes the appointment of information stewards, custodians and owners, and the beginning of governance groups and collaborative communities. Governance will

---

[22] Kaplan, R & Norton, D 2008, *The Executive Premium*, Harvard Business School Publishing Corporation, Boston, USA

also include putting the architecture and standards in place that will allow for proper approvals of AI and other technology tools that are required. It will also determine the way business and technology requirements are determined and maturity assessed, and what is required for any business cases that are required to fund the resources required for implementation of the strategy.

Establishing the appropriate technology is important and includes constructing the big data platform: starting at data capture right through to predictive and prescriptive analysis to proactively use data for decision-making.

The next chapter will cover the people stage of adopting the strategy as they are critical to executing the strategy. A skilled and capable workforce, that is open to automation and the use of artificial intelligence to achieve strategic goals, is essential for success. A successful organisational change program is required to transition people into the roles that are required. For medium to large organisations, data management and data science teams are essential with the specific skills and competencies that are required.

Processes will change dramatically with the execution of the strategy and the current process needs to be documented so that inefficiencies can be identified, and automation and workflow put in place.

The combination of governance, people, technology, process and the finance to enable initiatives will provide the ingredients to execute the strategy. It is necessary to review and refine the strategy at regular intervals and this is particularly important in the AI and data space where changes rapidly occur. Implementing an AI and data strategy is a major undertaking. It is not enough to hire a small team of data scientists and buy them analytics software to unleash the power of AI and data in the organisation.

Activities and Benefits

The strategy would not be complete without high-level activities and metrics linked to high-level benefits being identified to provide the necessary detail to obtain funding through business cases and initiate projects. It may be worthwhile to run a pilot or proof of concepts for AI and big data activities to establish quick wins before embarking on a major project.

Example Strategy

The final product of the strategy can come in various forms and the format is determined by the executive and the audience the strategy is being delivered to. Strategic Architects have produced videos, presentations, strategic overviews and detailed strategies to cater for the audience.

It is better to hold the workshops before the complete development of the strategy, to allow for input and suggestions so there is ownership of the strategy. From experience, it is useful to have some elements of the strategy defined first, as it can be difficult to run a strategy workshop from a blank page. It is also useful to have an area responsible for strategy realisation to ensure the strategy is being implemented and achieving the benefits and strategic outcomes.

The following strategic overview provides an example that brings together most aspects of the strategic architecture template for an AI and data strategy. The detail would come in an associated strategy document.

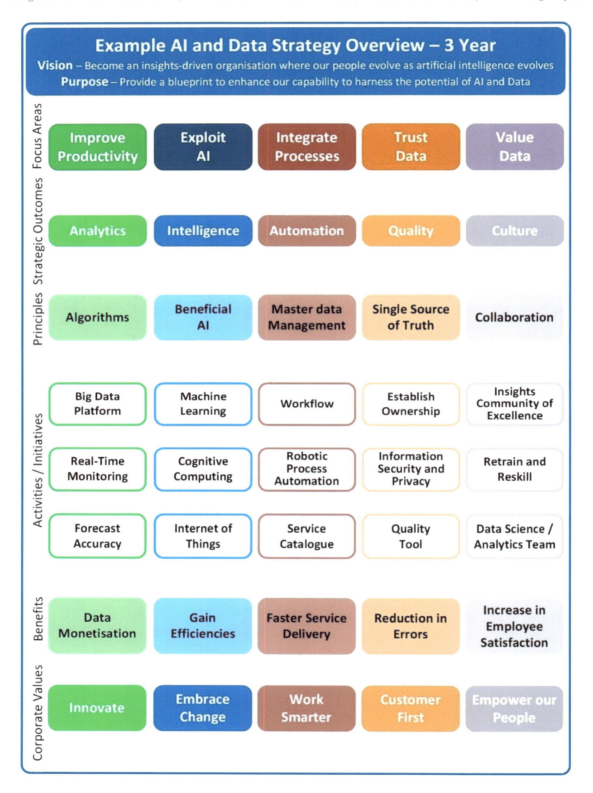

Figure 18: Example AI and Data Strategy

The AI and data strategy will be able to be measured instantaneously and updated progressively throughout the year, once real-time monitoring systems have been developed and data analytics leaders and teams can confirm the results.

One of the important decisions in determining activities to be included in the strategy is whether to outsource the activity. The main rule of thumb is if there is an existing capacity to undertake the activity in the organisation it may be worthwhile to enhance that capability. On the other hand, if there is no capacity the decision to outsource is much easier. For example, if there are no current Data Scientists, it would be difficult to justify financially the establishment of an entirely new team, at least initially until a pilot project was successful. In this situation, utilising a Data Science service through a consultancy firm may be the best option, providing potential risks like information security can be managed well. The next chapter and Chapter 5 will elaborate on the pros and cons of establishing new teams and transitioning staff to new roles. It is noted that for some emerging technologies like quantum computing it is likely that quantum computing as a service will be the best option to access this technology for several years for most organisations.

The next chapter considers how to establish a data culture in the organisation, as it is vital to have the people on board to transform the organisation into one that operates on factual data for decision-making, rather than gut feel.

Chapter 4: The Culture Transformation

In the last chapter we discussed the need for an AI capability driven strategy that identifies what is required in order to be best placed to take on future challenges. As vulnerable animals across the world become extinct, are we humans also vulnerable to becoming extinct in our workplace if we do not adapt, as digital disruption continues to transform how we manage our businesses today?[23] This chapter will explore how we align our culture with the organisation's AI goals to ensure we adapt in our workplace and embrace AI and data as a key resource.

What is an AI and Data culture driven organisation?

Historically business strategies were built from learnings and historical growth goals however, strategies can now be developed instantly from AI learning machines that provide key recommendations on future market, service and sales growth goals to improve predictability for success. AI will become key in optimising our business growth strategies and plans, but it lacks creativity. Business strategies can be measured instantaneously and updated throughout the year, by the data analytics leaders and teams who can confirm and interpret what is working and what isn't. Routine administration functions that don't add value will be replaced with more creative, empathetic and service driven functions from compassionate employees and teams.

AI enables leaders and employees to be become more accountable with measurable goals as humans and AI machines deliver business outcomes.   This involves understanding

---

[23] Tegman, M 2018, 'How to get empowered, not overpowered, by AI', *TED2018*, April, viewed 12 June 2019, <https://www.ted.com/talks/max_tegmark_how_to_get_empowered_not_overpowered_by_ai?language=en>

human values verses deep learning which together can assist with predictions and decisions.

An AI culture has leaders and employees who value data, embrace automation and accepts AI will enhance and complement existing services, products, markets and decision making. This includes a consistent, repeatable approach where strategic, tactical and operational decision-making is supported with empirical data analysis.

An AI culture will transform your organisation initially by replacing administrative paper processes and routine administration functions that don't add value with automation and digital processes so leaders and employees can focus on improving productivity and service delivery. By promoting a culture that analyses big data and automates complex processes together using AI, organisations will continue to modernise, adapt and grow with more insight driven outcomes. Organisations like Blockbuster video became extinct through digital disruption as the streaming of movies became popular through Netflix, together with the ability to download movies and TV shows from the internet.

Challenges of transforming to an AI and data culture

One of the complexities of establishing an AI and data organisational culture is the need to develop and hire employees with AI skills. However, due to the speed of AI transformation initiatives these roles and skills are not all readily defined and available in the marketplace. Only now in 2019 are universities offering a variety of new data science and data analytics masters, graduate diploma and undergraduate degrees across Australia and other countries. Hence the growth in AI capabilities and skills has had a slow start given the current huge appetite organisations have to invest in these capabilities.

The popularity of the Chief Data Officer (CDO) is increasing as they lead the transformation in building and maturing their AI capabilities into business as usual practices in the organisation. AI teams will need to be established which includes an equal number of technical, business, architects (AI, data, information and cloud), organisational change and customer experience staff who can develop programs that articulate how organisations can embrace an AI culture.[24]

New and startup companies find it easy to establish their digital teams as they develop, resource and deliver their AI strategy and plan. These organisations are using AI as the driving engine behind market analysis and service gaps to inform decisions whereas the traditional decision-making organisations find this a challenge and threat so they tend to ignore these insights. Traditional private companies and government agencies are yet to define their digital teams and resources and their existing structures are inefficient in developing modern digital funding and reporting models. Therefore, these traditional organisations are struggling to keep up with the digital age. The digital transformation is perceived as threatening and making it difficult for people to embrace the change.

By developing an AI and data culture, it will fundamentally drive in this new digital operational model where AI and people collaborate to get the best outcome possible for their organisation. The following figure shows a high-level model on how an AI and data culture can be defined so the underlying beliefs, assumptions, values and norms of both teams and employees can be transformed to embrace AI to modernise their social and psychological behaviors.

---

[24] Goasduff, L 2016, '3 Key Steps to a Data-Driven Business', *Smarter With Gartner*, 7 September, viewed 12 June 2019, < https://www.gartner.com/smarterwithgartner/3-key-steps-to-a-data-driven-business/>

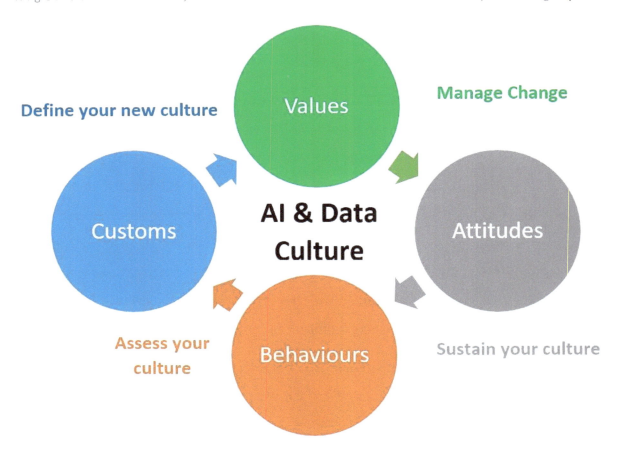

Figure 19: AI and Data Culture Transformation Model

Culture Change Model

Traditional organisational culture programs are established from shared values, beliefs and norms and habits that evolve among teams and employees through leadership and management.[25] These behaviours shape how the organisation achieves its strategy and historically is difficult to change in a timely manner. Therefore, a new AI and data culture change model is proposed from various culture theories to assist organisations in transforming their culture to align with their strategy and technical goals. The previous

---

[25] Aamodt, M 2003, *Applied Industrial/Organisational Psychology*, Wadsworth Publishing Company, Belmont, California, USA <https://www.amazon.com/Applied-Industrial-Organizational-Psychology-InfoTrac/dp/0534596886>

figure summarises this new model and how an organisation culture can be transformed efficiently into an AI and data culture where employees embrace technology.

The previous figure summarises how an organisation culture can be transformed into an AI data culture through four key stages:

1. Assess your culture
    a. This involves assessing the organisation's customs, norms and habits that drive employees' behaviours.[26]
2. Define your culture
    a. This involves defining and updating the organisation's values that enable employees to embrace and partner with AI and data resources.
3. Manage Change
    a. The key enabler to allow employees to transform to the new way of working.
4. Sustain your culture
    a. Enables the preferred culture change to be reinforced to continuously evolve towards the new way of working.

> Rio Tinto is leading AI culture transformation where they have the largest robot railway in the world in Western Australia where sixteen mines transfer iron ore to four shipping terminals using AI. They also use data-driven decision-making at their Weipa bauxite operations. Using their value-led approach they are continuing to transform their end to end value chain.

AI Culture Transformation[27]

1. Assessing your Culture

The first step in the model to establishing an AI and data culture, as shown in the previous figure, is to assess your culture by looking at the current norms, values, behaviours and

[26] Sherriton, J, Stern, J 1997, *Corporate culture, team culture: removing the hidden barriers to team success*, American Management Association, New York, USA, < https://www.worldcat.org/title/corporate-culture-team-culture-removing-the-hidden-barriers-to-team-success/oclc/34788587>

[27] 'What in the world do mining and rocket science have in coming?', RioTinto, Spotlight, blog posting 8 November 2018, viewed 13 July 2019, < https://www.riotinto.com/ourcommitment/spotlight-18130_26350.aspx>

whether people are contributing in a positive or negative way in their day to day roles.[28] Confirming these behaviours you can define how you can lead your workforce into a modern digitised organisation. Traditional gut instinct decisions will be challenged through deep learning machines and data insight outputs. One survey, reported by The Economist Intelligence Unit, confirmed this challenge when people were presented with data that contradicted their gut feel. Only 10% would take the course of action suggested by the data and 57% would reanalyse the data to hopefully get a response that was consistent with their intuition.[29]

By conducting a pulse survey, you can gain insights into your current state culture and what values and behaviours are driving your workforce culture. This is a quick way to gauge any AI and data values and behaviours. This will assist in determining the future norms, state values, behaviours and attitudes required to mature your organisation into becoming a modern digital driven business.[30]

An organisational culture includes the norms or customs that have become the habitual practices that employees undertake automatically with little thought. Change and uncertainty are key influences that drive a workforce culture. They can be a challenge to influence and change in traditional organisations but easy to establish in a new organisations. Changing these customs takes strong empathetic leadership, time and management, and employees need to have a logical reason for change that reduces feelings of uncertainty.

---

[28] Aamodt, M 2003, *Applied Industrial/Organisational Psychology*, Wadsworth Publishing Company, Belmont, California, USA, <https://www.amazon.com/Applied-Industrial-Organizational-Psychology-InfoTrac/dp/0534596886>

[29] Swabey, P 2014, 'Decisive Action: How businesses make decisions and how they could do it better', *The Economist Intelligence Unit 2014*, 5 June, blog posting, viewed 25 November 2018, <https://perspectives.eiu.com/technology-innovation/decisive-action>

[30] Vaus, D 2013, *Surveys in Social Research De Vaus*, Allen & Unwin, Sydney, Australia, <https://www.booktopia.com.au/surveys-in-social-research-david-de-vaus/prod9781742370453.html>

A pulse survey can be completed to assess where your current organisation culture is at, against key business drivers. These include:

Vision

An organisation's vision provides the direction of the company in terms of growth. It should be inspiring and lead to a positive staff perception of where the business intends to go. This vision will see people and technology collaborating to achieve the business vision.

Strategy

Sets the medium-term direction and how this will be achieved. For example, a strategy with high-level guiding principles on automation will enable flexible innovations to meet market uplifts and changes.

People

Provides the resourced skills and capability to deliver the vision and strategy together with the AI resources and capabilities.

Process

Processes will enable AI and people to work in collaboration to achieve growth and deliver on the strategy.

Execution

Execution includes the successful adoption and capability uplift where both people and technology work together to deliver the strategy and vision.

The following survey was developed for a relatively large service organisation who were looking to implement an AI strategy to reduce administration tasks so their employees could focus on improving their services.

No	Question	Driver
1	I am really excited about the future as we move to a digital AI organisation. ○————○————○————○————○ Strongly Agree Neutral Disagree Strongly Agree Disagree	Strategy
2	I understand how humans and machines will operate to meet the future business demands. ○————○————○————○————○ Strongly Agree Neutral Disagree Strongly Agree Disagree	Vision
3	My role will continuously change as we transform into a digital AI team. ○————○————○————○————○ Strongly Agree Neutral Disagree Strongly Agree Disagree	People
4	I regularly make decisions based on gut feel. ○————○————○————○————○ Strongly Agree Neutral Disagree Strongly Agree Disagree	Process
5	I can see how my creative ideas will work hand in hand with AI machines. ○————○————○————○————○ Strongly Agree Neutral Disagree Strongly Agree Disagree	Vision
6	Process automation is making my work life easier. ○————○————○————○————○ Strongly Agree Neutral Disagree Strongly Agree Disagree	Execution
7	I prefer to make decisions with data and facts. ○————○————○————○————○ Strongly Agree Neutral Disagree Strongly Agree Disagree	Process
8	I understand the importance of quality data to build digital AI capabilities. ○————○————○————○————○ Strongly Agree Neutral Disagree Strongly Agree Disagree	Execution
9	I can't see my current role in the future digital AI organisation. ○————○————○————○————○ Strongly Agree Neutral Disagree Strongly Agree Disagree	People
10	I can see machines and my team members working together to meet the day to day role activities. ○————○————○————○————○ Strongly Agree Neutral Disagree Strongly Agree Disagree	Strategy

The chart and table below provide a high-level summary of where of the survey results.

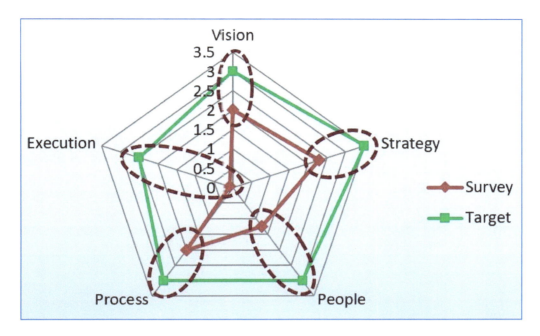

Driver	Survey	Target	Year 1 Target
Vision	2.75	4	3
Strategy	2.3	3.5	2.9
People	1.25	4	2
Process	2.9	3.5	3
Execution	0.09	3.5	3

Figure 20: AI and Data Pulse Survey Organisational Culture Results

2. *Define your New Culture*

The second step in transforming your culture is to define a new culture that is focused on how humans and machines work together until this becomes the norm. There is a famous quote that has been attributed (perhaps incorrectly) to Albert Einstein *'the definition of insanity is doing the same thing over and over and expecting a different result'.*[31] Therefore, when transforming into your AI culture this requires strategies, leaders, managers, supervisors and employees to update their shared values, beliefs and norms to achieve the day to day business goals. Workshops can be conducted to define the change journey required to transition to the future state. Creativity, transparency, quality, collaboration, sharing and recognition are all common strategic values for a modern digital data-driven organisation and selecting the most appropriate values are important.

Forrester research commissioned by Automation Anywhere found that 70% of survey respondents in ANZ businesses believed that their organisations have a position perception towards AI's Robotic Process Automation and actively managed the culture change.[32]

Most organisations have values defined and empower their people to uphold and live the values which are important when recruiting and retaining talent. What needs to be considered in building an AI and data culture are the values that drive behaviours to enable employees to embrace change, work smarter and innovate. These values, when accepted and championed, will encourage the changes needed to drive an AI and data culture. People have their own personal values and sometimes with the introduction of emerging technologies involving artificial intelligence, those personal values can be challenged. It is important to find a way to enable people to have their voice and be part of the transition as they establish new values aligned with any new organisational values.

The survey results shown previously from the service organisation showed that people felt threatened or uncertain about how AI would help them perform their roles.

---

[31] 'Albert Einstein in popular culture' 2019, Wikipedia, viewed 16 June 2019, <https://en.wikipedia.org/wiki/Albert_Einstein_in_popular_culture>

[32] Forrester Consulting 2019, 'ANZ Businesses Reap Early Success of RPA Adoption: Forrester Opportunity Snapshot: A Custom Study Commissioned by Automation Anywhere', Forrester Research, viewed 13 July 2019, <https://www.automationanywhere.com/images/lp/pdf/ANZ-business-reap-early-success-of-RPA-adoption.pdf>

Introducing values that reduce this threat and promote the opportunities of AI at an employee level will assist with this process. The second area for improvement was in the execution, which is not unusual as employees generally find it easier to sustain their current norms and behaviors than adopt new ones. This can take a few tries before they are fully embedded.

3. *Change Management*

The third step is to manage the change by enabling your employees to manage the AI machines, data and information effectively in their day to day roles. This is the most important step in the process and one that needs to be carefully planned. The change management plan will differ depending on the AI culture maturity of the organisation. It is very important to have executive support and buy-in, and to the flexibility to incorporate the changes they want as part of this sponsorship. The change management approach can be tailored depending on the current state culture. There are a range of existing resources in the marketplace that can assist.

An attitude is a belief which promotes how we behave in relation to something and can change over time as one grows and responds to the ever-changing world. Some attitudes can be about the 'best way to do things' and in a changing environment those attitudes will be challenged. In some situations, new staff with new skills - for instance, in the data science and analytics space, may be required where re-training staff is not an option. Over time these new staff can demonstrate new ways of doing things that are more efficient and may effect change in attitudes of existing staff.

A proper planned organisational change approach, led by the executive team is required to move towards a higher AI culture maturity.[33] By promoting collaboration and

---

[33] Smith R, King D, Sidhu R, Skelsey D, Busby N 2014, *The Effective Change Manager's Handbook: Essential Guidance to the Change Management Body of Knowledge*, The APM Group Limited, KoganPage, London, UK, <https://www.amazon.com.au/Effective-Change-Managers-Handbook-Management-ebook/dp/B00P6EW3V4>

information management, the sharing of successful decision-making cases can be very powerful as a change agent. Also, automating complex processes can save time, lead to less errors and provide timeliness of data so that quick corrective action can be undertaken.

The PROSCI ADKAR model is a popular change management approach used to move organisations from an old way of operating to a new one and is summarised as follows:[34]

1. Awareness - Is the first change phase, where employees are informed about the change, including the what, why, how and when it will occur. When employees understand the reasons for change, they can process and then confirm if they are going to embrace the change or resist it.

2. Desire - Is the next phase, which is recommended to enable organisations to provide some fun and excitement around the change to further influence their employees to embrace the change.

3. Ability - Involves employees learning new capabilities and is where they turn their knowledge into actions and behaviors as they learn how to manage the change in their day-to-day roles.

4. Reinforcement - Includes both the internal and external drivers that lead to the sustainability of the change. This includes benefit realisation, where employees see the value add for the organisation, as well as feeling of satisfaction as improvements in their day-to-day role are experienced.

4. Sustaining the Culture

The last step is maintaining the culture once established so that the people in the organisation don't fall into the trap of going back to old methods. Mapping the

---

[34] Hiatt J 2006, *ADKAR: A Model for Change in Business, Government and our Community*, Prosci Learning Center Publications, Colorado, USA, <https://www.amazon.com.au/ADKAR-Change-Business-Government-Community/dp/1930885504>

organisation's assets and allowing for data sharing can be a catalyst to keep progressing, learning and to maintain enthusiasm. Constantly focusing on reducing uncertainty and selling the benefits personally, as well as organisationally, will assist in maintaining your AI and Data Culture.

Chapter 5: Building an AI and Data Organisation

Understanding the Construct of an AI and Data Organisation

Without a suitable structure that provides the ability to unleash the power of AI and data, organisations will struggle to succeed with AI as most efforts will be siloed across different systems and business areas.

Leadership from senior executives in the organisation is important and the sponsor of AI and data activities could be a Chief Data Officer / Chief Analytics Officer / Chief Technology Officer / Chief Information Officer and/or Chief Executive Officer depending on the structure of the organisation.

Organisations differ in size and impact of AI and data. What is becoming more apparent is the need to have a specific team that undertakes the implementation of AI and Big Data for the organisation.

Strategic Architects specialise in providing advice on trends in AI and have a YouTube channel that has a series on AI Friday. Episode 3 discusses *'Skills for the Future'* that describes a number of technical, non-technical and people skills that are vital. Analytical, critical thinking and reasoning are obviously necessary but equally important in a well-balanced team is to have those with strategic, creative and communication skills to achieve the best results and have team harmony.[35]

There will be roles suitable for most organisations that are looking to maximise the use of AI and data and the following diagram and associated role descriptions are an example organisation structure for an AI and data team.

---

[35] Schmalkuche, N 2019, AI Friday Episode 3 – Skills for the Future, January, YouTube, viewed 10 January, 2019, Strategic Architects, Brisbane, Australia, <https://youtu.be/wSRgSGpVagg>

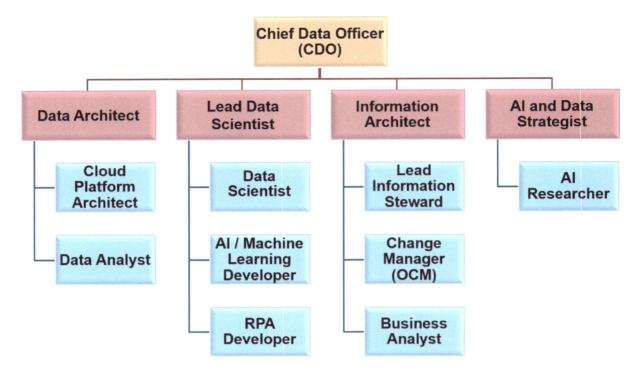

Figure 21: AI and Data Team

Chief Data Officer (CDO) – Executive level position that is responsible for the delivery of the AI and data strategy, manages the AI and data team and is responsible for the Big Data Platform. The CDO works closely with their team but also across the whole of IT and other parts of the organisation. There is a responsibility to analyse data effectively and for the data to be of a high quality. This needs to be communicated to everyone across the organisation.

Data/Information Architect – creates a blueprint for the AI/data organisation by designing, creating and managing the data organisation.

In larger organisations the CDO is critical and a Data Architect and an Information Architect is important. The Data Architect would develop the patterns and reference architectures for the development of the big data platform. The Information Architect would identify and secure information assets in collaboration with the cyber security and architecture teams. In smaller organisations where there is an AI/data aware CIO the management of the team could be delegated to the Data/Information Architect.

AI and Data Strategist – Formulates the AI and data strategy, aligns it to corporate strategies and communicates it to team and organisation and ensures implementation.

In larger organisations an AI and Data Strategist is vital, although an AI/data aware Enterprise Architect Strategist or Strategic Architect could fill this role.

Data Scientist – Modelling complex business problems and identifying opportunities using data mining and visualisation and the development of algorithms. Data scientists need to be curious and have strong mathematical and communication skills.

A data scientist is a mandatory role and there may be a need for a team of data scientists in larger organisations. They can be funded directly from the business areas, undertaking projects that deliver specific outcomes. McKinsey estimates that, by 2024, there will be 250,000 unfilled U.S. data science job openings[36]

There may be a need to have multiple data scientists with a Lead Data Scientist in place to manage the team as the role becomes more important to organisational success. A number of organisations have work experience and graduate programs for data scientist trainees. Where these programs are in place it is vital to have a Lead Data Scientist present to guide the development of Algorithms and co-ordinate and collaborate with the Data Analyst.

Data Analyst – Interprets patterns and trends in data to enable meaningful decisions to be made.

---

[36] McKinsey Global Institute 2016, *The age of analytics: Competing in a data-driven world,* December, viewed 9 February 2019, < https://www.mckinsey.com/business-functions/mckinsey-analytics/our-insights/the-age-of-analytics-competing-in-a-data-driven-world>

In smaller organisations the Data Scientist may undertake the Data Analyst role, however they would need to have the ability to interpret, which is an analytical skill. Most organisations will need a Data Analyst.

Organisational Change Manager – specialising in AI and data change to manage new business processes, organisational structure and cultural changes.

This is a vital role in all organisations and is responsible in delivering an AI and data culture in the organisation.

Lead Information Steward – Organises data sets across the organisation and ensures responsibilities and security is across all information.

Organising the data sets and ensuring they are of a high quality, secure and recorded once is a vital role. This role would need to co-ordinate with the cyber security specialists to ensure that security is across all data sets.

The following roles are optional depending on the maturity of the organisation:

Machine Learning Engineer – Designs and builds machine learning systems that solve problems and present solutions.

Machine Learning is becoming vital to all AI and data initiatives. This role can be undertaken by the Data Scientist in smaller organisations.

AI Researcher – Researches, collects, evaluates and provides advice, direction and information.

This role can be undertaken by the AI/Data Strategist or Strategic Architect (Enterprise Architect Strategist) in smaller organisations.

AI/Machine Learning Developer – Designs, develops, implements and integrates algorithms with software programs.

With the need for the development of algorithms, larger organisations will require a specialist in developing AI and machine learning. Smaller organisations would require the data scientist to undertake this role.

Cloud Platform Architect – Designs the big data platform and oversees it becoming operationalised.

The link between cloud, data and AI is important as the scale that can be provided by cloud is needed in all AI and data projects. Without this role the organisation would need to rely on discussions with the cloud/solution architects on the development of data lakes and data/insight cloud platforms.

Business Analyst – documents the business processes to undertake the implementation of AI and determines future business capabilities required.

There may also be a need for a Business Architect to compare current and future states, determine gaps and align with corporate strategy. Business Analysts can quite often be in the business areas and would need to discuss with the Information Stewards and Architects what the requirements from an organisational level are.

RPA Developer – Uses RPA tools that can automate processes. This is a specific role but is vital in industries where robotic processes are planned or being implemented for the organisation to optimise operations.

The roles listed are best in a central team (except Business Analyst) that can work in close proximity with one another. Attracting such extraordinary talent to your organisation can be difficult and virtual working environments with modern flexible workspaces is essential to attract employees with AI and data skills. It is vital that skill audits are undertaken across employees to establish upskilling programs and identify staffing skill shortages and opportunities.

Where a central team is established there would be a need for regular contact with business areas. Business areas will need to have information stewards to manage their data sets and business analysts to determine their requirements for data that may be provided by the central team through self-service. Involvement from right across the organisation is vital for the success of an AI and data organisation.

Establishing an Insights Community of Excellence

The analytics field is progressing towards the need for higher level discussions on insights to be the focus, rather than a conversation on technology tools, or how to report better in a more traditional manner. Strategic Architects have established several Communities of Practice from Artificial Intelligence, Business Intelligence and Reporting, to Advanced Analytics and Insight, learnt from the experience and can now share this knowledge with you.

Establishing a Community of Excellence can be a challenge and it is useful to have several important players to attend other organisation's communities where possible. Soft launches are useful to gain support and a groundswell before the proper launch with agendas and schedules. Early sessions need to include opportunities for members to suggest topics, commence and build on an Insights Register to monitor progress, and report back to senior management on success.

Communities of Excellence are a formal approach to establishing collaboration, but there are many other non-formal methods including encouraging collaboration through social media including Yammer, Facebook and LinkedIn. Other methods include hackathons to encourage innovation in the data/artificial intelligence area. With the changing face of the workforce in the future and the increasing proportion of millennials, that have never known life before big data exploded on the scene, people will demand an AI and data-driven culture and this may become a selection criterion when choosing which organisation they would like to work for.

The Insight focus for a Community of Excellence, requires a deeper discussion and it needs to be one that is led by the Chief Data Officer or Head of Analytics and Insights, to ensure the right level of discussion is undertaken at the right time for the organisation.

It has proven successful to have a map of the organisation's data and how it has been transformed into insights by the information owners. A good mix of information generated from the CDO's office, success stories, and significant time to share ideas, will result in an active community.

It is a significant effort to keep Communities of Practice or Excellence going and the right mix of senior staff, data evangelists and enthusiastic experts will help build the data-driven culture across the organisation.

Chapter 6: Realisation of Strategy

In the previous chapters, we discussed the need for an AI and data strategy within an organisation and a data-driven culture forms the spine of the strategy. In this chapter, we will dive into the aspects of critical activities and initiatives that will drive the momentum in realising the value and benefits assured by the AI and data approach.

'It is a capital mistake to theorise before one has data,'[37] said Sherlock Holmes. These words were true then, 100 years ago, true now and will remain true in the future. As data and information grow around us, the value extraction will be more beneficial than ever before. Not only does private enterprise today take note of the importance of data, but government and public sectors are also joining hands to create a data-driven economy. With everything revolving around digitisation, AI and data is more critical than ever before. But how do we make the transformation to the data-driven organisation? Success lies within an effective strategy and the execution of the strategy.

Most successful organisations decompose strategies into objectives, objectives into tasks and tasks into individual actions, in order to achieve business outcomes. This works perfectly well when all the employees are motivated at the same level and align with each other consistency. A business motivation model, as demonstrated in Chapter 2, is a good approach to drive this consistency and align the entire organisation to achieve business outcomes effectively. However, it is often challenging to keep the momentum going as sustained performance cannot be maintained without the right balance of human dynamics. Hence strategy execution requires a strong motivational leader who is well versed in balancing **People, Process, Data/Information and Technology** with a holistic

---

[37] Doyle, Sir A (Sherlock Holmes) 1891, *The Sign of Four*, A Scandal in Bohemia
<https://www.azquotes.com/author/4117-Arthur_Conan_Doyle>

view of how to mobilise the organisations resources to get the best investment value and outcome.

Often translating strategy into action relies on defining the right projects to develop and optimise the business capabilities by managing quality and investment priorities. Unfortunately, by their own admission, the majority of companies aren't very good at this well.

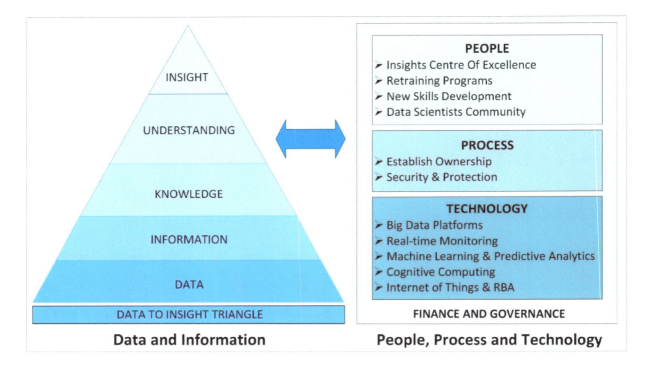

Figure 22: People, Process, Information and Technology Capabilities in AI and Data Initiatives

How can we ensure the realisation of the strategy?

The realisation of an AI and data strategy goes beyond mere ticking off the 'Big Data Platform' or 'Machine Learning' box. It requires careful selection of projects, collaboration with the right stakeholders and crafting effective skill management techniques. Instead of only focussing on short-term gains like cost optimisation or Return on Investment (ROI), include projects that involve new ideas, innovative techniques, performance improvement or those that can delight customers.

In Chapter 2, the capabilities of people, process, information and technology were introduced and discussed throughout the book as essential for capability-based planning. The previous diagram illustrates how to realise strategy through a focus on people, process and technology with governance and finance underpinning most of the new initiatives within an organisation. The other major element to realise the AI and data strategy is data and information and this is represented by the Data to Insight Framework (Triangle) considered throughout the implementation. The framework is important as it illustrates the transformation of data to insight that is required to realise an AI and data strategy. [38]

Following the development of the strategy, a high-level roadmap is produced with the initiatives mapped out against each strategic outcome. This has been done in a simple way in the following roadmap but does indicate the power of aligning initiatives against strategic outcomes to ensure project alignment to strategy.

---

[38] Schmalkuche, N & Swamy, R 2019, *Data to Insight*, Strategic Architects, Brisbane, Australia <https://www.amazon.com/Data-Insight-Transform-Actionable-Insights-ebook/dp/B07MJVH8ZL/ref=sr_1_2?keywords=Data+to+Insight&qid=1549683057&s=Books&sr=1-2>

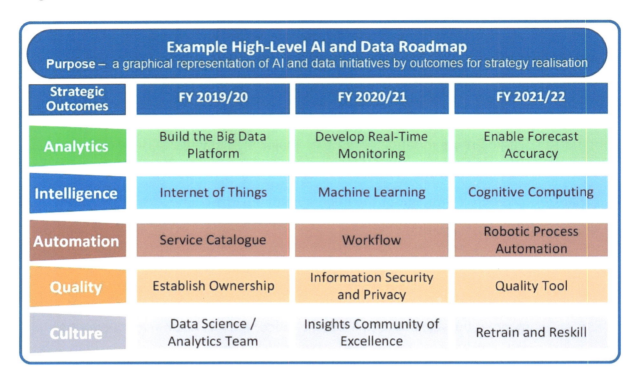

Figure 23: Example AI and Data Roadmap

Each of the three initiatives that are aligned to each of the strategic objectives, have for simplicity in this example, one major benefit. The following figure shows a portion of the strategy that illustrates this.

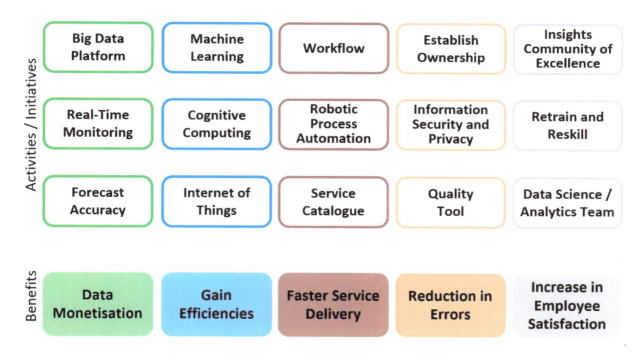

Figure 24: Example AI and Data Strategy – Implementation Section

Let's dive a bit deeper into the four areas of people, process and governance, technology and finance, to understand how they contribute to an organisation's AI and data strategy.

People

In Chapter 4, we discussed the critical need for organisations to develop a data-driven culture and Chapter 5 we discussed how to build an AI and data organisation. In this section we will build on the information presented in those chapters and discuss the implementation of strategy through the skilling of people in the organisation.

Most organisations wants to build a data-driven organisation. Data has long played a role in advising and assisting operationa and strategic thinking. An organisation invests into tapping data, which is the new black, the next logical step would be to build a strong team of data science and analytics. While that may sound easy it can be often challenging. The skills and capabilities which organisation should build within these teams include:

- Ability to find rich data sources

- Ability to work with large volumes of data despite hardware, software, and bandwidth constraints
- Ability to understand the data and meld the datasets together
- Building rich tooling that enables others to work with data effectively
- Analysing and visualising capabilities

The next challenge is of identifying data scientists and this can be challenge as there are not many who are properly trained. The number of analytics jobs and roles are increasing at a far faster pace than ever before. How can organisations create programs to build data-driven teams and achieve successful outcomes?

Retrain and Reskill

Currently, 80% of the data and analytics jobs created five years ago, are still not occupied, according to a study by the Wall Street Journal.[39] Hence instead of hiring, an option is to train within your employee pool. Teaching new skills and updating current skill sets in large teams might seem to be a Herculean task, but it is much simpler than we assume as the existing employees already have the required domain knowledge which makes the job half done. What they then need is training and skill development which allows them to apply complex analytics to existing problems. If some employees have the necessary background, then it makes sense to encourage them to upgrade their skills. Ultimately, a big data transformation is an enablement opportunity for the employees within an organisation to learn new skills, build expertise and stay relevant through times of disruptions.

Community/Centre of Excellence

Building a Centre of Excellence (CoE) means creating a shared facility that develops resources and best practices for big data processes. These CoEs could be cross-functional

---

[39] Digumarti, S 2016 'Gear your team for greatness in Data Science: Skilling and re-skilling your workforce', *Analytics India Magazine*, viewed 1 June 2019, https://www.analyticsindiamag.com/gear-team-greatness-skilling-re-skilling-workforce/

or even cross-organisational in nature. The more diverse they are, the more impact they will make on the program. If a group adequately includes subject matter experts, domain experts, or representatives from various business teams to help build models, this will provide encouragement to kick off the program. When building the CoE, cheerleaders are crucial, but naysayers and sceptics are equally important to keep a tab on the practicality of solutions and to keep the debate alive and valuable. Quite often, naysayers end up leading CoEs, becoming more passionate over time because, once their objections have been overcome, as they understand why the data transformation is so important.

Data Science and Analytics Team

Data science teams aren't just people: it's tooling, model building, processes and interaction between the teams and more. Data science teams can be centralised or distributed i.e. either they are IT-centric or distributed across the business units.

In an IT-centric model, the data science team takes complete responsibility for data preparation, training models, creating user interfaces, and model deployment within a corporate IT infrastructure. This is often led by the Chief Data Officer (CDO) or Chief Analytics Officer (CAO) within the organisation and is served through external vendor's "as a Service" to the business units. For example Machine Learning as a Service (MLaaS), Analytics as a Service (ANaaS) or even Data Science as a Service (DSaaS) models. This has many advantages as well as disadvantages.

Pros:

- Data is democratised leaving silo data models out of practice.
- One-time investment for the entire organisation.
- Reusability of machine learning tasks, skills and resources thus reducing the cost.

Cons:

- Limited machine learning methods and data consistency procedures that these services provide.
- The absence of domain knowledge may lead to generic models and thus yield limited or mediocre results.

Distributed Data Science Teams: In distributed data science teams, the data mining environment is distributed and so are the analytics and science teams. IT departments provide big data platforms either as Infrastructure as a service (IaaS) or Platform as a Service (PaaS). The intelligence and science team is distributed amongst the business units as domain experts are often sealed to their business functions. Here the leadership of data-driven programs falls on the shoulder of the Chief Executive Officer (CEO) of the organisation. Data democratisation has to be enforced as a policy in order to get the holistic picture of the insights. This model aids in addressing complex data science tasks that include in-depth research and use of multiple ML models tailored to assist their specific fields of analytical interest. The cons of such distributed data science teams include:

- Heavy investments into data science talent acquisition
- Data science talent engagement and retention challenges

Process

When an enterprise charts an AI and data strategy, organisations tend to transform themselves into data-driven enterprises. A comprehensive vision to enable data-dependant capabilities, starts to evolve out of technology transformation described above. In order to realise the big gains of data-dependant capabilities, processes are required to maintain efficiency and effectiveness of the strategy.

Data Lineage and Ownership

Data consumers are often faced with data governance challenges like:

- Who are data producers?

- Where can I find the required data?

- Who owns them?

- Who maintains them?

- Where can I find information on them?

- Is the information up to date?

- Who are the consumers of data?

This is an important feature of Information Architecture. Establishing data lineage and ownership becomes important even from the data governance perspective. Data lineage is a concept devised during the data extraction process, which means it is to note where the data came from. Data lineage also notes the data flow until the end of its lifecycle to provide history and origin for the user. Data lineage includes two sides - business (data) lineage and technical (data) lineage. Business lineage pictures data flows on a business-term level. This can be achieved through industry solutions like Collibra, Alation, etc. Technical data lineage is created from actual technical metadata and tracks data flows on the lowest level - actual tables, scr pts and statements. Technical data lineage can be achieved through solutions such as MANTA or Informatica Metadata Manager.

When it comes to establishing ownership, it comes from the principle that data is considered as an enterprise asset. In this scenario, the data owner holds the control and decides what information needs to be processed, providing meaning and context to the data. Any modification and enrichment to data fall under the responsibility of the data owner. When the data is critical, the security and protection of such data become critical. Below are some of the responsibilities defined for data owners:

- Supporting data consumers

- Authorisation of access and validation of security

- Data packaging and delivery

- Maintenance of data

- Management of business rules on data

- Metadata management

Although we can enumerate owner responsibilities as above, it does not help in assigning data ownership to one particular department or an individual. Hence it is important to understand who or where data will be best valued, managed and maintained.

Some of the steps of defining data ownership can be:

Step 1: Create a Data Ownership Policy

Step 2: Identify all the stakeholders both internal and external

Step 3: Create an enterprise Data Catalogue

Step 4: Identify and determine the roles

Step 5: Assign the ownership

Step 6: Keep record of ownership registry

Information Security and Privacy

Bruce Schneier's observation that 'security is a process, not a product'[40] in 2000 has been enormously influential in the security community. Since then, security has come a long way. There have been many radical changes in the technology landscape and is not expected to remain constant in the coming years. But what remains the same is the concept that security is not a product but a continuous process. In any data-driven organisation, one of the major concerns of the data is its security and privacy. The coordination and authorisation of access form part of this security process. If a system

---

[40] Schneier, B 2000, *Secrets and Lies: Digital Security in a Networked World*, Wiley Publishing, Indianapolis, Indiana

carries corporate intelligence or highly confidential information, it becomes all the more necessary to define a security and authorisation policy.

It's very rare that enterprises deploy their AI and big data environment on-premise. Most of them are cloud-based. Hence, they are faced with different types of privacy and security issues from regular data centre challenges. Hence data-driven organisations follow some key principles in order to maintain their security posture.

Principle 1: Security is key - involve the team right from the beginning.

Security is not an afterthought when it comes to designing big data platforms. They have to be prioritised right from the beginning of the data processes. Often the security team is viewed as obstructionists by the data project teams and so are brought in very late. But by then it would usually be very late to put in any meaningful security measures to adequately secure the environment. The big data team must recognise its commitment to incorporate robust security measures into its environment, even if it decelerates their technology plans.

Principle 2: Keeping the end in mind.

Before prescribing the usual security measures that teams are accustomed to, security teams can begin keeping the end goal in mind. Once the business objectives and their purpose for consuming analytics are known, security teams can customise the design to meet the business requirements and risks. If the security team is involved very late in the development stage, backward security engineering comes into play. Security teams can start off by understanding what the objective of analytics within the organisation are and then apply tactical measures to manage the risk. Also, enterprises have to realise that a big data environment cannot be made secure through the implementation of one security product, but multiple products and efficient processes.

Principle 3: One-size doesn't fit all.

There is no one-stop shop for big data security. Big data technologies are a collection of multiple technologies stitched together to chart the data journey within the organisation. Data typically flows throughout an enterprise from many sources/applications, through various data integration services, and into many target repositories. Hence security has to be ensured throughout its journey and at its rest. That makes creating a security solution complicated. Start by identifying security risks at each stage and then customise a stack of tactics to address the risks identified at the beginning of the process.

Security is always an uphill battle, but the organisations that are the most successful employing AI and data strategy are the ones that form a true partnership between the data and security teams and commit to developing a customised and objective-driven resolution.

Data Quality

Deciphering data and getting an insight is only as good as the quality of the data. Bad data quality impacts every aspect of an enterprise. Quality management is an important Data Governance function which is often owned by the business, with roles and responsibilities shared with IT. Some of the tools that can ensure data quality are data discovery tools, data profiling tools and data monitoring tools. Although data quality is more of a governance process than a technology aspect of big data, some tools can reduce data errors and improve data quality.

Since big data is a collection of diverse data sets from disparate sources, it is difficult to measure the data quality. To make data quality dimensions measurable, trackable and auditable, the below two-layered dimensions can be incorporated. Layer-one represents the characteristics that make data effective and credible; layer-two represents the elements within the dimension that strengthens the character.

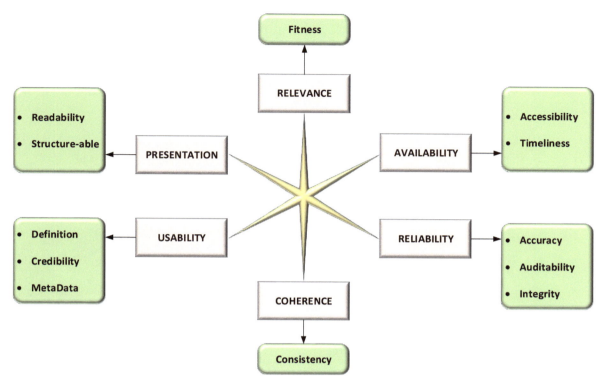

Figure 25: Data Dimensions

In the above figure, the inner layer has six inherent characters of good data and the outer layer represents the elements that build those characters. Mastering the understanding of data quality measures and keeping the above key characteristics in mind will ensure enterprises establish a solid DQM (data quality management) foundation.

Information (and Data)

The data to insight triangle represents 'information' out of the people, process, information and technology capabi ity model.

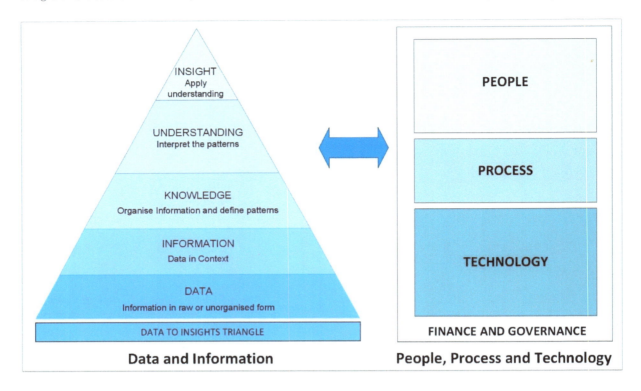

Figure 26: People, Process, Information, Technology for AI and Data Summary

Information (and data) is represented by the summary version of the data to insight triangle above and is central to the other capabilities including people, process and technology in an AI and data strategy. There is a need for a coordinated effort across all the areas of the data to insight triangle, to deliver the AI and data strategy. The data layer includes the capture and store of data in an unstructured or structured form. The information layer provides context to the data, and the knowledge layer is where the information is organised and patterns are defined. In the understanding layer patterns are interpreted so that meaning is attached.

Gaining Insight is the application of that understanding to a useful endeavour. The capacity for experts to combine their knowledge with the resources of AI leads to better decisions being made.

For more information please refer to Chapter 1, Data to Insight, that discusses the application of capabilities for the AI and data strategy and Strategic Architect's earlier book named 'Data to Insight'.[41]

Technology

Technology plays a crucial role when it comes to interactions with customers and being able to strategise the next business goal. By examining the current technical capabilities, organisations can gauge how they can be made more efficient to extract valuable outcomes. Artificial Intelligence purely depends on data and the interactions of algorithms, so when it comes to AI and data strategy, success is largely dependent on robust data and analytics infrastructure.

Big Data Platform

Building a big data platform starts with an understanding of what data is required to achieve the business outcomes or gain insights. A good understanding of data types and sources will often form the foundation for strategic decisions like "Build or Buy the platform" decision or even to figure out data acquisition and ingestion strategies. Traditional capabilities like a data warehouse and local data marts still play a crucial role in descriptive and diagnostic analytics. In order to develop Predictive and Prescriptive analytical capabilities, the analytical infrastructure needs to be re-examined. Architecting an analytical platform requires many parties at the table, including data experts, leaders in technology, and business and subject-matter experts. Above all, having executive leader support that drives the AI future passionately is important to be able to support the resources required to develop the platform. Hence getting your team ready and building your foundation would be the first step towards the strategy.

---

[41] Schmalkuche, N & Swamy, R 2019, *Data to Insight*, Strategic Architects, Brisbane, Australia, <https://www.amazon.com/Data-Insight-Transform-Actionable-Insights-ebook/dp/B07MJVH8ZL/ref=sr_1_2?keywords=Data+to+Insight&qid=1549683057&s=Books&sr=1-2>

Once the buy or build decision has been realised, proceed in equipping the platform with data discovery tools. Develop reusable reference architectures and patterns for data ingression or egression from various sources. Re-evaluate the business intelligence layer for advanced analytics, in-database statistical analysis, advanced visualisations above regular reports and dashboards. Set up a scorecard to monitor milestones and measure capabilities being built.

Real-time analytics and Forecast Accuracy

Of late, there has been a lot of progress with real-time monitoring utilising Internet of Things. AI-driven analytics has powered real-time monitoring, analytics, and operations. There have been a number of case studies across a number of domains where real-time insights are fuelling innovative ways of doing business. Understanding the need for real-time analytics within one's organisation will enable the organisation to build a strategy-focused implementation model. Real-time analytics incorporate analytics that bring real-time insights and real-time context to the decisions. With a platform that can process the streaming data with near-zero latency reduces the time to insight. This involves capturing streaming data, filtering, aggregating, enriching, and analysing with prebuilt algorithms that can identify simple and complex patterns. This can provide applications with context to detect anomalies and automate immediate actions, and dynamically adapt. Real-time analytics on constantly changing data requires different skills and a different mindset. Many industry leaders like IBM, Google, Oracle etc. provide streaming solutions along with some machine learning capabilities. If instead, there is a requirement for a completely customised environment specifically designed for their domain, it can be built from scratch utilising Apache Spark or Apache Flink. The three criteria to be kept in mind while building a real-time analytics platform are as below:

- Keep the capacity and velocity requirements of streaming data into consideration while architecting the Platform solution. This means even frontend infrastructure should be adequately provisioned to handle high-velocity data.

- Not just the bandwidth, incoming transactions must also be handled at significant volumes. Ensure your in-memory databases are adequately sized. Also, by quickly identifying and moving unneeded data from memory to long-term storage, querying latency can be dealt with.

- The idea of a distributed architecture, where many smaller machines do smaller jobs to complete a bigger job faster, makes sense in real-time analytics. Carefully sizing and batching how the data is distributed across nodes, and also separating processing into smaller jobs can help to do a lot more with data as it comes in.

> The opportunities for the gains of real-time analytics and forecasting within Big Data is different depending on the industry. One such application of Big Data analytics is in obtaining accurate weather forecasts. But it is interesting to note how a fashion industry like EDITED (https://edited.com/data/) is using Big Data for forecasting the fashion future by collecting data from social media. Using advanced machine learning, EDITED's data scientists have not only taught their systems to do more than access and collect information, but have also taught them to understand what they're looking at and make predictions at real-time.

More Data. With More Data Science Behind It[42]

Machine Learning

Machine learning is a core part of AI that provides computer systems with the ability to automatically learn and continually improve based on that learning without human programming.[43] Computers can analyse data, learn from the data and information in the form of observations and continuous real-world interaction.

---

[42] Edited 2019, *More Data. With More Data Science Behind It*, blog posting, viewed 30 June 2019, <https://edited.com/data/>

[43] Schmalkuche, N & Swamy, R 2019, *Data to Insight*, Strategic Architects, Brisbane, Australia <https://www.amazon.com/Data-Insight-Transform-Actionable-Insights-ebook/dp/B07MJVH8ZL/ref=sr_1_2?keywords=Data+to+Insight&qid=1549683057&s=Books&sr=1-2>

Machine learning consists of algorithms that can automate analytical model building. Building these models requires thoughtful consideration of which business problems and challenges we are trying to solve and what data is available at hand. Marrying the data to business problems through algorithms calls for careful selection and assessment of test and training datasets. Using algorithms that iteratively learn from the training dataset, they provide some hidden insights from the data without explicitly programming the code. Some of the ways to realise the machine learning capabilities within the organisation are:

- Start with simple models: Building an intricate ML model to extract insights from the data is crucial, however, simple models are easier to deploy, test and explain to the stakeholders through data storytelling. The common saying *'Rome wasn't built in a day'* definitely applies to the building of algorithms. With complex models, it is hard to triage if any problems arise. The first few models are ideal to concentrate on as low hanging fruit and hence simpler models will provide that required start and boost as quick wins and the foundation for going forward. In the initial phases of strategy realisation, the organisation focuses on platform infrastructure. It is only after technology infrastructure is ironed out that designing algorithms and building complex models will become easier. In establishing Machine Learning, thinking big while starting small is the key.
- Detect glitches and hotspots: Before moving your models to production, ensure complete testing is done to check anomalies especially due to oversampling or under sampling. If there is a hotspot found in training datasets, users may not notice them outright. This may lead to the corruption of test data. If there are lingering issues with data itself, don't export the model to production.
- Use multiple models or combination models: Data scientists usually use one or two models per problem, often commonly used algorithms. These models might fit better than others for that particular dataset, but the combination of models

or multiple algorithms can do a better job of capturing specific spaces of your training data.

- Plan the iterative approach never assume that the model deployed today would stay relevant in months to come. Remember the complexity or new objectives that are being added to the existing model. Re-examining models and developing new features will maintain currency.

> *Netflix House of Cards started on February 1, 2013, was licensed by Netflix based on the analysis and data gathered by Netflix. They have observed that viewers who liked House of Cards were a fan of Kevin's films and liked the movies directed by the David Fincher. They have algorithms to predict and understand the views preferences so they bet on Licensing House of Cards which turned out to be accurate. It is remarkable to note that Netflix spends $1 billion purely on the development and management of its algorithms.*

Data as a Secret Weapon[44]

Cognitive Computing and Internet of Things

Internet of Things (IoT) has already started playing a crucial role in shaping the future of many organisations across various domains, from agriculture to manufacturing, and healthcare industries. The combination of IoT and Cognitive Computing have the power to leapfrog the efficiency levels, improve business models and eventually surge ahead in competition. When Internet of things goes hand in glove with Cognitive computing the impact on the industry will be incredible. Let's see what Cognitive Computing is and how organisations can leverage this capability to unlock the huge potential of AI and Data. Cognitive Computing involves technologies like machine learning, deep learning, neural networks, NLP (Neuro-Linguistic Programming) and sentiment analysis to mimic human thought processes. Internet of Things plays a very crucial role by collecting the data for analysis so that models and algorithms can be developed to help draw insights. Imagine

---

[44] Petraetis, G 2017, 'How Netflix built a House of Cards with big data', IDG Communications, Inc., *CIO*, blog posting, viewed 30 June 2019, <https://'www.cio.com/article/3207670/how-netflix-built-a-house-of-cards-with-big-data.html>

an appliance that can sense the weather and transform the workplaces and homes to the optimal temperature settings, or anticipate maintenance issues helping people to plan alternatives before they culminate into events. Cognitive systems like IBM Watson are designed to help an organisation keep pace, serving as a companion to enhance its workforce's performance. The main goal of the Internet of Things is to connect more closely with the physical world through things. It shares information about the physical world that includes the cars we drive, the tools we use, and the buildings we live in. However, without cognitive computing, the usefulness of all the information would be limited by its own complexity and scale. Here are four steps to building Cognitive Computing:

- The first step in building Cognitive Computing capability within the organisation is to look for the opportunities that align with the business strategy. Define the solutions that commit to the business benefits and fund the solution implementations that address the business challenges.

- In order to identify the use cases present in the organisation, involve business stakeholders and define the problem statements accurately. This helps in designing the hypothesis required for building AI models. Involving business resources helps you to fine-tune the models precisely for solving business challenges.

- The third step is to foster experimentation within the organisation. AI and data strategy within an organisation must be complemented with innovation. Constant testing and validation of models for use cases identified not only keeps the momentum going, but also provides a new understanding of the data.

- Deploy the cognitive solution even if it doesn't completely solve the business problem as greater learning is enabled when people involved in designing and training the models improve the algorithm. Continuous learning, continuous improvements, and exploration of further use cases for the application of

Cognitive Computing in the organisation is crucial. Keep track of business benefits through defined metrics helps to sustain the enthusiasm within the projects.

As an organisation moves toward an AI and Data-driven future, it's vital to remember that cognitive computing is a journey and this journey evolves over time.

> *NEC's NeoFace Watch solution is specifically designed to integrate with existing access control and surveillance systems by extracting faces in real time from existing video surveillance systems and matching against a watch list of individuals. When the system identifies an individual of interest from the watch list, it raises an alert, so appropriate actions can be taken rapidly to reduce the risk of public safety threats.*

Know the Face in the Crowd[45]

Robotic Process Automation, Workflows and Service Catalogue

Robotic Process Automation (RPA) is a process of automating manual routine task procedures existing within an organisation. Business practice shows that the costs of high-volume manual tasks are enormous for companies. These processes can be automated with software robotics and artificial intelligence. Realising RPA strategy within the organisation is similar to building Cognitive Computing capability within an organisation. This includes identifying business challenges, ensuring stakeholder confirmation on use cases, and experimentation and innovation through continuous improvement. The real challenge of RPA within the organisation is to build a business case that can justify the requirements and benefits of RPA. Below mentioned are some of the use cases that can prove to be a path-breaking idea for elevating the RPA business case.

---

[45] NEC 2019, *Know the face in the Crowd,* blog posting, viewed 30 June 2019, <https://www.nec.com.au/expertise/safety-security/identity-access/facial-recognition/neoface-watch>

- **RPA with Artificial Intelligence for help desk software**: RPA tools usually depend on structured data, static rules and repeatability of tasks. But to handle unstructured data and dynamic rule sets, artificial intelligence is required. For example, making use of Artificial Intelligence (AI) and Robotic Process Automation (RPA) to create helpdesk chatbots can interact with human customers to offer an immediate, natural, and intuitive response to common customer problems and questions.

- **Simple Automation:** The use of sophisticated artificial intelligence software to automate repetitive tasks which otherwise take human staff time can be converted into software bots releasing their time to more creative tasks.

- **Data Extraction**: Data entry is a nightmare of monotony for your employees. A good Optical Character Recognition or Pattern recognition AI software can help enterprises convert any kind of text into editable and searchable machine-encoded text which drastically reduces the need for manual data entry. This not only frees up employee time for more challenging work but also creates fewer human errors with faster and better results.

- **Accounts Reconciliation**: Accounts reconciliation is mostly performed to ensure records are error-free. Software robots can perform activities like data extraction from bank statements and compare records and reconcile purchase orders with delivery notes within minutes.

- **Customer Service Operations**: Simple, repetitive, high-frequency tasks like making customer profiles or billing data available and updating customer profiles can be automated through software bots thereby reducing customers' waiting time and allowing employees to focus on human-specific jobs like communication and public relations.

The list above is not limited to finance and operations, but also can be extended anywhere where repetitive tasks can be automated through algorithms and software bots.

When launching a new theft ID insurance program, Shop Direct Group Financial Services successfully utilised a Process Automation solution. The company was able to use a library of process components within an RPA solution which allowed them to quickly automate the customer-registration process. Blue Prism's Digital Workforce allowed Shop Direct to rapidly bring this popular new product to market. Additionally, the automation saved them the time and effort of hiring and training 22 additional employees.

Process Automation Solution[46]

Finance

There are many crucial challenges for businesses in their mission to grow and create data-driven teams, align culture, and manage costs along with their business strategy. Finance needs to play a critical role in ensuring organisations continue to thrive through this transformational journey of realising their AI and data strategy. This requires investment in new practices, technologies, and skills that increase the business' capacity to adapt at pace. Finance can help the organisations by developing a pragmatic model for business partnering for insights, identifying the mechanisms for cost-effectiveness without compromising the AI journey and identify growth opportunities through this transformation.

Organisations are constantly looking to reinvent themselves to stay in the competition. There's never been a better time for the reign of the data economy. From economic pressures that demand greater efficiency to new kinds of products that weren't conceivable a few years ago, the opportunities presented by AI and big data are tremendous. It's not easy to build a data-driven organisation, but if it were easy, it

---

[46] Blue Prism© 2019, Shop Direct Supports Product Launch with Blue Prism, blog posting, viewed 30 June 2019, <https://www.blueprism.com/resources/case-studies/shop-direct-supports-product-launch-with-blue-prism>

wouldn't trigger so much excitement in combining the talents of individuals to achieve the strategic outcomes documented in the AI and data strategy.

Chapter 7: Benefits Realisation

Benefits of Adoption an AI and Data Strategy

AI and data are changing the way businesses are run. Even though many companies are launching data-focused businesses, very few have achieved significant financial impact, which requires the right combination of strategy, culture, and programs. Let us look at the benefits of adopting an AI and data strategy.

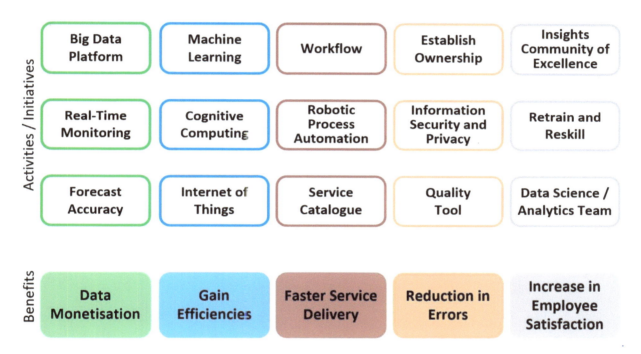

Figure 27: Example AI and Data Strategy – Implementation Section

Data Monetisation

Some organisations are moving towards data monetisation as it is rapidly becoming a differentiator especially in financial sectors, energy markets and in some sections of the public sector. The foundation of data monetisation is comprised of the building blocks made up of data and analytics. If companies are confident of their strategy and analytics, and the talent within the company, they can effortlessly monetise the data they have invested in. Some of the ingredients required for data monetisation are:

Strategy: A successful strategy execution plays a crucial role.

Leadership and culture: Successful data-and-analytics programs require real commitment from business leaders, along with a consistent message from senior leaders on the importance and priority of these efforts.

Innovation: Innovative solutions and service packaging to provide unique datasets often give organisations a competitive edge.

Commitment: Efforts to monetise data are more effective when they are business-led and focused on the most valuable use cases. Hence equal commitment from all parts of the organisation is important, as imbalance will lead only to obstacles and failure.

> *Grocery retailer Kroger captures shopping data generated by its rewards card and sells it to consumer packaged-goods companies thirsty for a deeper understanding of their customers' shopping habits and evolving tastes and preferences.*
>
> *AkzoNobel, a Dutch multinational company, has created a decision-support model for ship operators to enable fuel and CO2 savings. They make available to ship operators and owners an advanced analytics-enabled mobile iOS app that provides continuous performance prediction of coating technologies. This approach empowers vessel operators by allowing financial and performance benefit analysis of coating choices, thus optimising important investment decisions.*

Demystifying Data Monetisation[47]

Operational Efficiencies

Jim Hare, research vice president at Gartner, made the following observation, *"AI offers exciting possibilities..."*[48]. Gaining operational efficiency is a never-ending quest for many organisations. They constantly look for innovative methods to improve efficiency in order to revolutionise the customer interactions. At the heart of every business, there are critical systems and processes driving operations across functions. AI's multi-facets like machine learning, image and video analysis, speech recognition and natural language processing can be utilised to increase sales, improve customer satisfaction, and produce company insights. But before getting carried away with the shiny machine learning technologies on offer, thinking about the pain point an organisation is trying to address for its customers is the best way forward to gaining efficiencies. Only then, should one proceed considering if and how any of AI's manifestations can improve the organisation.

---

[47] Gandhi, S, Thota, B, Kuchembuck, R, Swartz, J 2018, 'Demystifying Data Monetization', *MITSloan Management Review*, blog posting, 27 November, viewed 30 June 2019, <https://sloanreview.mit.edu/article/demystifying-data-monetization/>

[48] Moore, S 2017, 'Gartner Says AI Technologies Will Be in Almost Every New Software Product by 2020', Gartner Newsroom Press Release', viewed 1 June 2019, <https://www.gartner.com/en/newsroom/press-releases/2017-07-18-gartner-says-ai-technologies-will-be-in-almost-every-new-software-product-by-2020>

Taking baby steps and solving one problem at a time can be the best way forward for AI and data beginners in achieving operational efficiency.

Figure 28: Object and Scene Detection – 'Honey – The family dog'

The previous picture shows the use of Amazon Rekognition software[49] for object and scene detection. Other vendors like Microsoft Azure (Computer Vision), Google (Vision AI) etc. utilise machine learning in a similar way. The software automatically labels objects, concepts and scenes in your images, and provides a confidence score. The confidence level for the object in the picture to be a golden retriever was 98.8%. There was no programming required to achieve this result. All that was needed was to establish an AWS account, upload the photo of 'Honey – the family dog' and allow the software to utilise the capability that has been achieved. It is likely that there has been 1000's of dog photos over a period of time used to train the machine learning technology to be able to

---

[49] 'Amazon Rekognition' 2019, Amazon Web Servers, blog posting, viewed 13 July 2019, <https://aws.amazon.com/rekognition/>

achieve this result. Other software can be used to identify the age of the dog and other details.

Improved Service Delivery

Improved customer service is increasingly needed across almost every industry, the service industry perhaps most of all. Reducing waiting times and getting it right first-time in any service delivery plays a significant role in enhancing customer satisfaction. With technologies like IoT, mobility and predictive analytics, many organisations are moving from reactive to proactive service mechanisms. Beyond improvements in the field, IoT can provide unprecedented data about devices and their use. Equipped with AI and machine learning based solutions, service providers can collect and turn the vast amount of data collected about customers and service interactions into action and drive meaningful improvements.

The latest customer surveys have indicated that customers give equivalent weighting to the quality of the product and their experience of making the purchase. By studying a customer's behaviour in various stages of the buying cycle, big data analytics has enabled companies to improve the customer experience they offer. To provide the best customer experience the digital platform should address customer queries in the order they are likely to be asked. We have explored how robotic process automation can help the customers in this function. Also, by using behavioural analytics, companies can analyse customer behaviour, determine their pain points and restructure the digital platform and reach-out mechanisms to suit their needs. A smooth service delivery experience is all that is needed to ignite a desire and stimulate interest in purchase.

Amazon is one of the biggest companies in the world and artificial intelligence and the use of deep learning technology has been central to building their on-line business. Traditionally, one of the disadvantages of online shopping is the delay in receiving goods. By using predictive analytics, Amazon are able to determine buyer behaviour by the clicks and the searches that are made by shoppers on the internet. Anticipatory shipping is a faster solution for on-line businesses as it ensures products are available at a close geographical location to the buyer. If the customer orders the product the delivery time is then shortened and buying is made more attractive. A more aggressive strategy is to use drones to deliver the product based on buyer behaviour without the customer ordering the item. It will be interesting which strategy is the most successful over the longer period and there is no doubt that the building of algorithms will be a central part in the improvement of service delivery and customer experience.

Anticipatory Shipping through the use of Predictive Analytics[50]

Increased Customer Satisfaction

As Artificial Intelligence is making its way into business processes across organisations, one of its greatest impacts can be seen in the customer experience arena. With the advent of digitalisation, customers now have access to a tremendous amount of information about products and their substitutes. Customers suddenly have a variety of choices available and information on each product is easily available. Hence companies are in the fierce competition of retaining a customer base whilst tapping the new markets. Customer experience has become key to winning this battle. For some companies AI and big data have come to the rescue to help them maximise the level of customer experience they offer.

With the use of big data and artificial intelligence, companies are able to offer products and services that consumers are most likely to purchase. These are mostly possible

---

[50] Ulanoff, L. 2014, 'Amazon knows what you want before you buy it', *Predictive Analytics Times*, blog posting 27 January, viewed 6 July 2019, <http://www.predictiveanalyticsworld.com/patimes/amazon-knows-what-you-want-before-you-buy-it/>

through the use of recommendation systems. With the vast data of customer history, preference, price range of purchase, interests, etc., the artificial intelligence is able to recommend products and services customers may be interested in. With the use of AI and big data, companies can penetrate the markets at an individual customer level.

These benefits are essential when procuring AI and data technologies to ensure that the organisation can achieve their strategic goals. Amazon CEO Jeff Bezo recently said on stage, at his company's inaugural *'re:Mars artificial-intelligence and robotics conference'* on 7 June 2019, that the true secret to business success is to focus on the things that won't change, not the things that will. *"What can we do to offer lower prices? To deliver faster? and so on"*.[51] Even a company so progressive and innovative as Amazon ensures that they maintain their focus on delivering efficiently to their customers.

AI and Data Benefits Dependency Map

The following Benefits Dependency Map for an AI and data strategy has been developed to provide an example of how benefits can achieve the strategic objectives of the organisation. The strategic drivers represent the senior management's views as to what is important and where the change is required to occur and exist independently of any initiative. The strategic objectives are the success criteria for a change initiative. [52]

---

[51] Bort, J 2019, 'Jeff Bezos says the true secret to business success is to focus on the things that won't change, not the things that will', *Business Insider Australia – Tech Insider*, 7 June, Viewed 8 June 2019, <https://www.businessinsider.com.au/jeff-bezos-asks-himself-simple-question-when-planning-for-future-2019-6>

[52] Jenner, S 2014, *Managing Benefits*, APMG-Business Books, Buckinghamshire, UK <https://apmg-businessbooks.com/books/project-programme-management/managing-benefits-second-edition-2014>

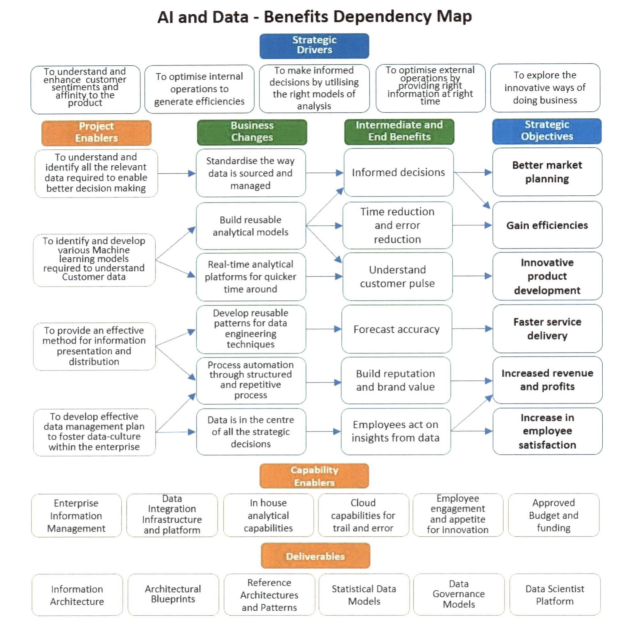

Figure 29: AI and Data – Benefits Dependency Map

Conclusion

The potential of AI and data technologies is in no way limited to the above-mentioned benefits. Helping businesses, from potential customer identification to after sale services, AI and data can improve the efficiency of business in every sphere. With the induction of an AI and data strategy, companies can reach out to customers easily when required, where required. The evolution of AI and data is turning out to be an inevitable necessity for businesses striving for sustainability and the essential ingredient to surge ahead of competitors.

.

Epilogue

The Fourth Industrial Revolution, as the current convergence of all things digital is often called, is set to dramatically change our world. Artificial Intelligence, Machine Learning, Autonomous Vehicles, Robotics, ... when we link together massive amounts of (digital) data, powerful algorithms and sheer unlimited computing power, and combine this mostly virtual world with the material world we live in, who knows what the future will look like?

Nobody knows for sure. Much of what our future looks like will be decided by the decisions we make today. We have many choices to make and many possible roads to consider. One choice we don't have, whatever line of business we are in, is to ignore all those changes, sit still and hope they will pass us by. We will have to adopt, adapt and transform in order to survive. The world we do business in radically changes, so our business will have to do the same.

What I hope you learned from reading this book is that, even though the future is uncertain, you don't have to blindly find your way forward. It has been said that "the best way to predict the future is to create it" and this book shows you, in a clear and methodical way, how to set about and do just that.

It starts with creating and detailing a vision: a guiding statement of what you want the future of your business to be. Inspired and informed by the enormous potential for improvement and transformation of almost all elements of business, your vision should be bold and daring. It is the ticket to your desired destination; in a future you are co-creating. But a vision without the capability to make it happen is just wishful thinking. And that is where this book really comes into its own. To be able to create your own digital future, AI and data have to become strategic business capabilities: core capabilities of your future business, rather than interesting technologies, or tools to play around with.

Out of all that is out there you will have to select the technologies, platforms and methodologies that best match your envisioned future. You will have to identify the skills and expertise needed to build that future. And then craft your strategy and tactics, step by step, following the advice, examples and templates presented in this book, to take you all the way to execution and benefits realisation.

What the book also clearly demonstrates is that you cannot treat AI, ML and Data as technologies you can simply add to your existing business and expect them to be successful. These technologies are transformational and require deep changes to your business models, processes, organisational structures and culture to deliver. This means that a successful AI and data strategy is at its heart a people strategy: it needs to be based on an understanding of how your people can be inspired, guided and supported to acquire the necessary skills, adopt a data mindset and culture, and embrace rather than resist the many changes this will bring to their work environment.

The biggest mistake you could make in your AI and data strategy is to assume that your people are just there to implement and maintain the technologies and platforms. Or that the function of AI, ML and Data Analytics is to replace expensive and unreliable humans with cheap and predictable machines. Sure enough, AI and related technologies have the potential to relieve humans of a lot of repetitive, analytical, dangerous and uninspiring work. However, for a long time to come, machine intelligence will be limited in scope and application because it lacks certain crucial human capabilities.

Humans can show empathy: the ability to not just reason from another person's perspective but also feel what that person experiences. Humans have the creative ability to jump out of their own frame of reference and come up with truly innovative ideas and solutions to existing problems. Humans have the 'meta-reasoning' capability to recognise when their existing knowledge and experience produce unexpected and potentially harmful results. This allows them to stop in their tracks, reconsider, and try a different approach. And humans can give sense and meaning to events and information in a way that makes sense to themselves and other humans. As long as we live in human world, you will need humans to bring empathy, creativity, innovation, resilience and - most important - a human touch to your businesses.

You also need more from your people than just showing up and doing their work; you actually need them at the best of their capabilities, with the right skills and mindset, and fully inspired and motivated to contribute the best they are capable of. Only with the full engagement of your people can you expect to realise the full potential of the promises AI and data have to offer. That means that an important part of your AI and data strategy must focus on the culture in your organisation. With the right strategy, the right culture, the right mindset and the right motivation, you won't have to wait for the future to happen to you. Instead you will be defining that future as you redefine your business and transform your organisation for success.

Bard Papegaaij

References

- 'Albert Einstein in popular culture' 2019, Wikipedia, viewed 16 June 2019, <https://en.wikipedia.org/wiki/Albert_Einstein_in_popular_culture>
- Aamodt, M 2003, *Applied Industrial/Organisational Psychology*, Wadsworth Publishing Company, Belmont, California, USA <https://www.amazon.com/Applied-Industrial-Organizational-Psychology-Infotrac/dp/0534596886>
- Bermejo, C, Huang, Z, Braud, T and Pan H 2017, 'When Augmented Reality meets Big Data', *In Proceedings of the Annual IEEE International Conference on Distributed Computing Systems (ICDCS 2017) - HOTPOST'17 workshop*, Atlanta, GA, USA, June 5-8, viewed 11 November 2018 <http://www.cse.ust.hk/~panhui/papers/carlosBermejo_hotpost_2017.pdf>
- Blue Prism© 2019, Shop Direct Supports Product Launch with Blue Prism, blog posting, viewed 30 June 2019, <https://www.blueprism.com/resources/case-studies/shop-direct-supports-product-launch-with-blue-prism>
- Bort, J 2019, 'Jeff Bezos says the true secret to business success is to focus on the things that won't change, not the things that will', *Business Insider Australia – Tech Insider*, 7 June, Viewed 8 June 2019, <https://www.businessinsider.com.au/jeff-bezos-asks-himself-simple-question-when-planning-for-future-2019-6>
- Bostrom, N 2014, *Superintelligence: Paths, Dangers, Strategies*, Oxford University Press, London, UK
- Casado, R and Younas, M 2014, 'Emerging trends and technologies in big data processing', *Concurrency and Computation, Practice and Experience*, 1 October, viewed 1 March 2019 <https://onlinelibrary.wiley.com/doi/abs/10.1002/cpe.3398>
- Cascade 2018, *Strategic Planning 101*, blog posting, viewed 20 November 2018, <https://www.executestrategy.net/blog/strategic-planning-101-the-basic-foundations/>
- Curran, S 2018, *3 Fundamental Steps for Strong Big Data Security*, viewed 7 April 2019, <https://tdwi.org/articles/2018/02/06/dwt-all-3-steps-for-strong-big-data-security.aspx>
- Diamandis, M 2016, 'Massive Disruption Is Coming with Quantum Computing', SingularityHub, viewed 7 April 2019, <https://singularityhub.com/2016/10/10/massive-disruption-quantum-computing/#sm.00000qjucssaijfq5sb1lyehubw9u>
- Digumarti, S 2016 'Gear your team for greatness in Data Science: Skilling and re-skilling your workforce', *Analytics India Magazine*, Viewed 1 June 2019, https://www.analyticsindiamag.com/gear-team-greatness-skilling-re-skilling-workforce/

- Doyle, Sir A (Sherlock Holmes) 1891, *The Sign of Four*, A Scandal in Bohemia, <https://www.azquotes.com/author/4117-Arthur_Conan_Doyle>

- EA Learning 2019, *Applied Business Architecture Course*, viewed 2 June 2019, <https://www.ealearning.com/our-courses/courses/applied-business-architecture.html>

- Edited 2019, *More Data. With More Data Science Behind It*, blog posting, viewed 30 June 2019, <https://edited.com/data/>

- ElonMusk 2014 'Worth reading Superintelligence by Bostrom. We need to be super careful with AI. Potentially more dangerous than nukes', August 3, Twitter Post, viewed 1 March 2019 <https://twitter.com/elonmusk/status/495759307346952192>

- Forrester Consulting 2019, 'ANZ Businesses Reap Early Success of RPA Adoption: Forrester Opportunity Snapshot: A Custom Study Commissioned by Automation Anywhere', Forrester Research, viewed 13 July 2019, <https://www.automationanywhere.com/images/lp/pdf/ANZ-business-reap-early-success-of-RPA-adoption.pdf>

- Foster, R 2012, 'Big data and public health, part 2: Reducing unwarranted services', *Healthcare IT News*, May, Viewed 22 June 2019, <https://www.healthcareitnews.com/news/big-data-and-public-health-part-2-reducing-un-warranted-services>

- Gandhi, S, Thota, B, Kuchembuck, R, Swartz, J 2018, 'Demystifying Data Monetization', *MITSloan Management Review*, blog posting, 27 November, viewed 30 June 2019, <https://sloanreview.mit.edu/article/demystifying-data-monetization/>

- Gartner Newsroom 2018, *Gartner Says Global Artificial Intelligence Business Value to Reach $1.2 Trillion in 2018*, press release, Gartner, Stamford, Connecticut, 25 April, viewed 10 February 2019, <https://www.gartner.com/en/newsroom/press-releases/2018-04-25-gartner-says-global-artificial-intelligence-business-value-to-reach-1-point-2-trillion-in-2018>

- Goasduff, L 2016, '3 Key Steps to a Data-Driven Business', *Smarter With Gartner*, 7 September, Viewed 12 June 2019, < https://www.gartner.com/smarterwithgartner/3-key-steps-to-a-data-driven-business/>

- Jenner, S 2014, *Managing Benefits*, APMG-Business Books, Buckinghamshire, UK <https://apmg-businessbooks.com/books/project-programme-management/managing-benefits-second-edition-2014>
- Kaplan, R & Norton, D 2008, *The Executive Premium*, Harvard Business School Publishing Corporation, Boston, USA <https://www.amazon.com/Execution-Premium-Operations-Competitive-Advantage/dp/142212116X>

- Kosner, A 2014, 'Tech 2015: Deep Learning and Machine Intelligence Will Eat the World, *Forbes*, Dec 29, viewed 3 February 2019, <https://www.forbes.com/sites/anthonykosner/2014/12/29/tech-2015-deep-learning-and-machine-intelligence-will-eat-the-world/#1114fad05d94>

- Institute for Quantum Computing 2018, *University of Waterloo*, blog posting, viewed 11 November 2018, <https://uwaterloo.ca/institute-for-quantum-computing/>

- Lewis, M 2016, 'How Two Trailblazing Psychologists Turned the World of Decision Science Upside Down', *Vanity Fair HIVE*, 14 November, viewed 4 November 2018, <https://www.vanityfair.com/news/2016/11/decision-science-daniel-kahneman-amos-tversky>

- Loshin, D 2001, *Enterprise Knowledge Management*, Elsevier Science and Technology, San Francisco, USA, <https://www.bookdepository.com/Enterprise-Knowledge-Management-David-Loshin/9780124558403>

- Marr, B 2017, *Data Strategy*, Kogan Page, London, UK

- Marr, B 2019, *Artificial Intelligence in Practice*, Wiley, Cornwall, UK <https://www.amazon.com/Artificial-Intelligence-Practice-Successful-Companies/dp/1119548217

- McKinsey Global Institute 2016, *The age of analytics: Competing in a data-driven world,* December, viewed 9 February 2019, < https://www.mckinsey.com/business-functions/mckinsey-analytics/our-insights/the-age-of-analytics-competing-in-a-data-driven-world>

- Moore, S 2017, 'Gartner Says AI Technologies Will Be in Almost Every New Software Product by 2020', Gartner Newsroom Press Release', Viewed 1 June 2019, <https://www.gartner.com/en/newsroom/press-releases/2017-07-18-gartner-says-ai-technologies-will-be-in-almost-every-new-software-product-by-2020>

- Nation's Manpower Revolution 1963, *United States Congress*, U.S. Government Printing Office, Washington, USA

- NEC 2019, *Know the face in the Crowd*, blog posting, viewed 30 June 2019, <https://www.nec.com.au/expertise/safety-security/identity-access/facial-recognition/neoface-watch>

- Object Management Group® 2015, *Business Motivation Model* v1.3, April, Viewed 23 June 2019, <https://www.omg.org/spec/BMM/1.3/PDF>

- Peters, J 2016, 3 Ways 3D Printing and Big Data can work together, *SmartDataCollective*, <https://www.smartdatacollective.com/3-ways-3d-printing-and-big-data-can-work-together/>

- Petraetis, G 2017, 'How Netflix built a House of Cards with big data', IDG Communications, Inc., *CIO*, blog posting, viewed 30 June 2019,

<https://www.cio.com/article/3207670/how-netflix-built-a-house-of-cards-with-big-data.html>

- Piletic, P 2019, 'Augmented Reality – The Future of Advertising', *Datafloq©*, blog posting, viewed 20 July 2019, <https://datafloq.com/read/augmented-reality-the-future-of-advertising/3333>

- Roberts, J 2016, 'What is HoloLens? Microsoft's holographic headset explained', Trusted Reviews, blog posting 30 March, viewed 5 July 2019, <https://www.trustedreviews.com/opinion/hololens-release-date-news-and-price-2922378>

- 'Robotic process automation' 2019 , Wikipedia, viewed 9 February 2019, <https://en.wikipedia.org/wiki/Robotic_process_automation>

- Schmalkuche, N 2019, AI Friday Episode 3 – Skills for the Future, January, YouTube, viewed 10 January, 2019, Strategic Architects, Brisbane, Australia, <https://youtu.be/wSRgSGpVagg>

- Schmalkuche, N & Swamy, R 2019, Data to Insight, Strategic Architects, Brisbane, Australia <https://www.amazon.com/Data-Insight-Transform-Actionable-Insights-ebook/dp/B07MJVH8ZL/ref=sr_1_2?keywords=Data+to+Insight&qid=1549683057&s=Books&sr=1-2>

- Schneier, B 2000, *Secrets and Lies: Digital Security in a Networked World*, Wiley Publishing, Indianapolis, Indiana

- Schwab, K 2017, *The Fourth Industrial Revolution*, Portfolio Penguin, London, UK

- Sharma, V 2017, How quantum physics can make encryption stronger, TED@Westpac, December, viewed 11 November 2018, <https://www.ted.com/talks/vikram_sharma_how_quantum_physics_can_make_encryption_stronger>

- Sherriton, J, Stern, J 1997, *Corporate culture, team culture: removing the hidden barriers to team success*, American Management Association, New York, USA, < https://www.worldcat.org/title/corporate-culture-team-culture-removing-the-hidden-barriers-to-team-success/oclc/34788587>
- Simmhan, Y & Perera, S 2016, Big Data Analytics Platforms for Real-Time Applications in IoT. <https://link.springer.com/chapter/10.1007%2F978-81-322-3628-3_7>
- Smith R, King D, Sidhu R, Skelsey D, Busby N 2014, *The Effective Change Manager's Handbook: Essential Guidance to the Change Management Body of Knowledge*, The APM Group Limited, KoganPage, London, UK, <https://www.amazon.com.au/Effective-Change-Managers-Handbook-Management-ebook/dp/B00P6EW3V4>
- Swabey, P 2014, 'Decisive Action: How businesses make decisions and how they could do it better', *The Economist Intelligence Unit 2014*, blog posting 5 June, viewed 25 November 2018, <https://perspectives.eiu.com/technology-innovation/decisive-action>

- Tegman, M 2018, 'How to get empowered, not overpowered, by AI', *TED2018*, April, Viewed 12 June 2019, <https://www.ted.com/talks/max_tegmark_how_to_get_empowered_not_overpowered_by_ai?language=en>

- The Open Group 2018, *The Open Group Standard, The TOGAF Standard, Version 9.2*, The Open Group, <https://www.opengroup.org/togaf>

- Ulanoff, L. 2014, 'Amazon knows what you want before you buy it', *Predictive Analytics Times*, blog posting 27 January, viewed 6 July 2019, <http://www.predictiveanalyticsworld.com/patimes/amazon-knows-what-you-want-before-you-buy-it/>

- Vaus, D 2013, *Surveys in Social Research De Vaus*, Allen & Unwin, Sydney, Australia, <https://www.booktopia.com.au/surveys-in-social-research-david-de-vaus/prod9781742370453.html>

- 'What in the world do mining and rocket science have in coming?', RioTinto, Spotlight, blog posting 8 November 2018, viewed 13 July 2019, <https://www.riotinto.com/ourcommitment/spotlight-18130_26350.aspx>

Index